Destination Louvre

A guided tour

**Collection
Chercheurs d'art**

**Catherine Boulot
Violaine Bouvet-Lanselle
Françoise Broyelle
Marie-Thérèse Genin
Jean-Marc Irollo
Daniel Soulié**

LOUVRE
Service culturel

Ⓜ Réunion
des Musées
Nationaux

Summary

The Louvre consists of seven departments, each one represented by a colour. The colours identifying the departments are to be found at the top of each page in this guide.
Some of the departments are sub-divided into collections (French paintings, Italian paintings, French sculptures, foreign sculptures ...).

Each room bears a number – more rarely a letter, sometimes a historical name is added.

Oriental antiquities

Egyptian antiquities

The Louvre palace

Decorative arts

Sculpture

The pyramid

Entrance to the museum is through the pyramid "transparent and reflecting the sky" as its creator, the American architect of Chinese origin, Ieoh Ming Pei, described it.

The spiral staircase leading down to the Hall Napoléon, departure point for many excursions through one of the biggest museums in the world, is also the work of Pei.

Characteristics of the Pyramid: 21.64 metres high; 35.40 metres: dimension of one side of the base; weighs 200 tons of which 105 of glazing and 95 tons of steel girders; 75 diamond-shaped and 118 triangle- shaped panes of glass. A tracked robot was specially designed for its weekly cleaning.

We offer you a continuous itinerary through the Louvre which will enable you to have a comprehensive view of the departments whilst making for the principal works.

Just in one visit this would last too long, we suggest you break up your tour and make several visits. Or you may decide to visit the Louvre collection by collection.

This itinerary suggests the shortest way of going from work to work, sometimes to the detriment of chronology. Maps and explanations are there just to help you find the way.

The Hall Napoléon

Take the escalator marked "Richelieu". Turn right after the ticket control to start your tour at the entresol, by a visit to the Islamic Art Collection belonging to the Department of Oriental Antiquities.

The Richelieu wing was built between 1852 and 1857 under Napoléon III; it borders the rue de Rivoli. Between 1871 and 1989 it was used by the Ministry of Finance. This wing of the palace, completely refitted on four levels, was inaugurated during the bicentenary of the Louvre museum in 1993. Today the Louvre is entirely devoted to works of art.

Cour Napoléon:
Statues of the Great men of France

Celestial globe

In less than a century after the death of the prophet Mohammed (632), the Arabs established themselves on a very large territory, spreading from Spain to India. Different populations were converted to Islam: Iranians, Turks and Berbers, contributing later to the creation of Muslim civilization. The immense empire, fruit of the first conquests, broke up very rapidly. Multiple dynasties were created, but over and above regional diversities, Islam, the common religion, remained a unifying influence.

Classical antiquity imagined the universe as interlocking spheres: on the fixed spheres, stars were unalterably positioned. Constellations were defined by sketched outlines and identified with mythological figures. Islam took up these conceptions and confirmed them by arithmetic and the observation of the works of Greek astronomers, in particular those of Ptolemy.

This "map of the sky" was traced on two brass half-spheres; 48 constellations are accompanied by their name; the stars are indicated by different sized silver points and are numbered according to an alphnumeric system. The most important are followed by their name; one of the graduated lines represents the ecliptic, a zone crossed by the sun in its annual course and which corresponds to the signs of the zodiac. This celestial globe is the oldest oriental example on which the constellations are shown.

Celestial globe
signed by Yunus Ibn
al-Husayn al-Asturiabi
Iran, probably Isfahan,
1144
Hammered brass with gold and
silver inlay – D 0.19 m

The Baptismal Font of Saint Louis

After their victory over the crusaders and the Mongols, the Mameluke sultans of Cairo dominated the Near East. For more than two centuries, the prosperity of their Empire is reflected in the architecture of their capital and the production of lavish objects, often of a very large size.

Large bowl known as *the Baptismal Font of Saint Louis*
Egypt or Syria, late 13th-early 14th century
Brass engraved and inlayed with gold and silver – D 0.50 m

Metal crafts were at their zenith. This large bowl with its remarkable decoration is signed in six places by Muhammad ibn Zayn. It is made of a single sheet of hammered brass with gold and silver inlay. The outer surface illustrates a procession of dignitaries and servants, interrupted by circles of princes on horseback. Two animal friezes (lions, leopards, gazelles, elephants and unicorns) run round the top and the bottom. The font used to be kept in the Sainte-Chapelle in Vincennes. It was used for the baptism of certain princes from the royal family, in particular during the nineteenth century; that is why the French coat of arms can be seen inside the font.

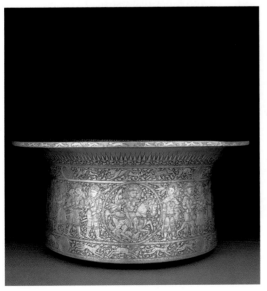

Carpet called "from Mantes"

Mantes carpet, detail
North-western Iran
late 16th century
Wool – L 7.83 m; W 3.79 m

In the vast room 11, objects from Central Asia, Iran and India are displayed.

Made in Iran under the Safavids in the sixteenth century, this famous carpet comes from the collegiate church in Mantes, and is one of most beautiful known. In the centre a panther is ready to jump on an antelope and around them a fight has started between a dragon attacked by two phoenix. There is also a garden, birds, antelopes and a lion slaughtering a gazelle, while a hunter in a turban aims his musket at a lion. This careful, colourful decoration reminds one of a miniature.

Peacock dish
Turkey, 1540-1555
Siliceous ceramic with a painted
and glazed decor – D 0.375 m

Richelieu 3
Entresol
room 12

Room 12 is devoted to the Ottoman world. Coming from a modest Turkish tribe, the Ottoman dynasty was founded towards 1300. Enlarging its territory little by little, it consolidated its power in 1453 with the taking of Constantinople, which then took its present name of Istanbul. The town became the capital of an immense empire spreading from Hungary to the Caucasus and Algeria. The Ottoman court had a taste for luxury and extravagance and lived in a sumptuous and colourful setting. It reached its zenith under Suleyman the Magnificent (1520-1566).

Ceramic was especially appreciated. Potters in the large centre of Iznik produced objects – dishes, goblets, large bowls and ceramic wall coverings. The palette of colours used became richer and richer throughout the seventeenth century. On this dish of refined tones – blue, mauve-grey, lime-green – a peacock evolves gracefully in the midst of a large bouquet.

After room 13 of the Islamic section, go up the Colbert staircase as far as the ground floor to visit the Oriental Antiquities. Rendezvous, straight ahead in room 1.

Richelieu 3
Ground floor
room 1a

Tablet with pre-cuneiform writing
Djemdet-Nasr, Late 4ᵗʰ century BC.
Clay – H 4.6 cm

It was in Uruk, in the country of Sumer, that writing first appeared, in 3300 BC. It was first of all invented for counting harvests and animals. The Sumerians traced the picture of the object they wished to designate on a clay tablet; these images are called pictograms.

In this room may be seen tablets dating from the 4ᵗʰ millenium BC. Further on, other tablets show the evolution of writing. Cuneiform writing – this word comes from the Latin cuneus, which means "corner" or more exactly *nail* – uses letters in the form of corners. It was difficult for the writer to make curves in the soft clay with a bull-rush. On the other hand, it was easier to write by stamping corners or nails into the clay tablets.

Mesopotamia, Iran and the Levant made up the Orient of ancient times which reached from the Mediterranean Ocean to India. For more than five thousand years, many civilizations followed one another. The oldest began in Mesopotamia "the country between the rivers", between the Tigris and the Euphrates (Irak and a part of Syria today). Surrounded by arid deserts, it included a large plain fertilized by alluvium, where agriculture and cattle-rearing flourished. For centuries, the country was coveted, invaded, destroyed and then reconstructed, because of its natural resources.

Richelieu 3
Ground floor
room 1a

The *Stele of Vultures* (c. 2450 BC) was erected by Eannatum, King of Lagash, in Mesopotamia, commemorating his victory over the neighbouring town of Umma; this battle cost the lives of "thirty six thousand enemies" (a symbolic figure). It is one of the earliest historical documents to have reached us. The monument was built to glorify the king's exploit, and even if the context is religious, it foretells the concept of the divine rights of royalty of future eras. The text and illustrations are displayed on both sides of the monument: the "historical" side shows the facts; the "mythological" side offers a symbolic picture of the victory.

The stele of vultures
The mythological side, detail.
Tello c. 2450 BC
Limestone – H 1.80 m

The Superintendant Ebih-II

The royal city of Mari, situated on the present frontier between Irak and Syria, witnessed the rise of a refined Sumerian-influenced civilization around 2500 BC. Excavations which began in 1933 brought to light a palace and several temples dating from the 3rd century BC. In the temple of Ishtar, goddess of Love and War, remarkable statues were found, proving the riches of the city.

Perfection was attained in the sculpture of Mari with *Ebih-II, the Superintendant of Mari*. This Chancellor of the Exchequer is represented as a sitting figure with crossed hands. The translucent alabaster in which he is sculpted lends great subtlety to the statuette. The eyes still possess their shell and lapis lazuli inlays, encrusted in schist. Like Eannatum he is clothed in a kind of woollen skirt (kaunakès).

Richelieu 3
Ground floor
room 1b

Ebih-II, Superintendant of Mari
c. 2400 BC
Alabaster, eyes inlaid with
shell and lapis lazuli – H 52.5 cm

The Stele of Naram-Sin

Sargon was the first monarch to forge an empire by uniting Sumer, Akkad and northern Mesopotamia. His son Manishrusu and his grandson Naram-Sin succesfully held this empire together, thus creating favorable conditions for a politicized form of art chiefly concerned by the image of the all powerful monarch, whose palace was at Agade.

The art of Agade reached its zenith under the reign of Naram-Sin (2254-2218 BC), its masterpiece being this stele in pink sandstone which offers a striking glimpse of the prince, followed by his army, climbing a mountain covered with astronomical and divine symbols. He is at the head of his soldiers, taller than all of them, wearing a horned helmet, a sign of his divinity. Indeed, Naram-Sin declared himself divine during his lifetime. He trampled the corpses of the defeated. The peak in front of him symbolizes "the mountain of hell" where he precipitated his enemies. This is an important historical document: an inscription in Akkadian language tells of the victory of the king over the mountain people of Zagros (western Iran); another in Elamite, added in the twelfth century, informs us that the stele was taken to Elam at this time.

The Victory Stele of Naram-Sin
Susa, c. 2280 BC
Standstone – H 2 m

Richelieu 3
Ground floor
room 2

13

Black silhouettes of different sizes, seated or standing but with their hands always crossed and wearing the same headpiece, fill room 2. Certain are merely fragments while others are complete. It is always the image of the same sovereign: Gudea, who reigned over the State of Lagash, in southern Mesopotamia, towards 2120 BC.

One statue shows him bearing a vase that "spouts water". In many ancient civilizations, water symbolized life. The inscription on the Prince's robe is a dedication to Geshtinanna, whose name means "celestial vine".
The statues reunited here were intended to perpetuate the Prince's prayers to the gods.
He wears a long fringed robe of linen and a wide-brimmed hat which, like the crown in our civilization, signifies royal or princely power. Gudea's face is idealized: the sculptor has designed his eyebrows in the "shape of fishbones".

Richelieu 3
Ground floor
room 2

Gudea with a spouting vase
Tello, c. 2120 BC
Dolerite – H 0.62 m

The Law-Codex of Hammurabi is one of the most remarkable works in the Louvre. It is one of the most ancient collection of laws in the history of mankind. The stele was erected by Hammurabi, king of Babylon between 1792 and 1750 BC. The king is depicted at the top of the stele, in front of Shamash, the solar god of Justice. The king wears a wide-brimmed royal headpiece and flames are spurting from his shoulders. He is holding a sceptre and a ring, signs of his divine power. All around the stele, two hundred and eighty two laws are written in an elegant cuneiform character. The different laws concern the family, marriage, divorce, adoption, inheritance, theft … For example, "if someone steals the god's belongings (in a temple) or from a palace, so shall that man be killed". The epilogue well resumes the spirit of the text. "Such are the just sentences that Hammurabi, a wise king, made in order that his country be well-disciplined and well-behaved".

Richelieu 3
Ground floor
room 3

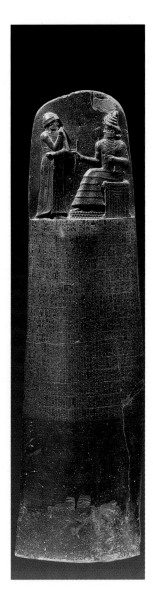

*The Law-Codex
of Hammurabi*
1792-1750 BC
Basalt – H 2.25 m

15

The palace of Sargon II at Khorsabad

In the vast courtyard which opens out to the right are presented the impressive remains of the palace of Sargon II at Khorsabad.

Between 713 and 705 BC, the powerful Assyrian King Sargon II (721-705) had a magnificent and imposing palace built in northern Mesopotamia, in Khorsabad. It spread over almost 10 hectares.

It consisted of courtyards and rooms, the walls of which were covered in murals (over two kilometres of murals in all). The setting of the palace was to glorify Assyria, its king and its gods. The gates of the building were guarded by winged bulls with human heads, more than 4 metres tall. These five-legged animals seem to have only four legs when looked at from the front or the side.

Great heroes, who were also lion-tamers, protected the palace. Let us look at one of these giants: bearded and wearing long hair, dressed in robes with heavy fringes, he is shown here choking a lion. He personifies strength and courage, kind towards guests of the palace yet terrifying to his enemies.

Richelieu 3
Ground floor
room 4

Winged human-headed bull
Palace of Sargon II,
End of the 8th century BC
Gypsum – H 4.20 m

The reliels on the walls of the Palace of Sargon II represent processions of dignitaries and servants, such as those advancing towards the portal of the throne room, or the parade of the defeated bringing their tribute to the king.

Other murals show the transportation of cedarwood from the Lebanon to Khorsabad to build the palace (since there was no wood in Assyria). The timber was transported by light vessels, the prows of which were decorated with a horse's head, on a sea evoked by stylized wavelets, fish and tortoises. The stories are told from right to left: timber felling, carrying it to the boats, crossing the sea, – the arrival at the palace, is shown at the top, on the left. Mythical creatures assumed protection of the vessels; human-headed bulls, winged bulls, magical fish …

A hero mastering a lion
end of 8th century BC
Gypsum previously painted – H 4.50 m

To leave the courtyard, go between the two bulls placed under the vault. Turn right and go straight ahead till you come to room 7.

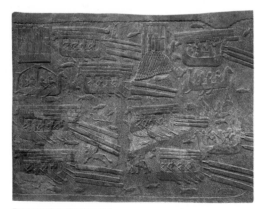

Transportation of cedarwood from the Lebanon
North wall of the great court of honour of the Palace of Sargon II, end of 8th century BC
Alabaster – H 3.08 m; W 4.09 m

The Ibex goblet

From room 7 to
room 16 objects
from Iran are on
display. Iran consists
of a vast group of
mountains divided
into districts of
several areas:
the mountainous
regions of Zagros
and Luristan, for
example, and the
plains, such as the
area of Susa, a natu-
ral extension of the
Mesapotamian plain.
Original cultures
began here, enriched
by exchanges with
neighbouring
Mesopotamia and
the Orient.

In Iran at the end of the fourth millenium BC appeared an important urban
civilization.
The capital city of Susa, founded
towards 4200 BC has left us important
archeological remains from different
periods. Painted ceramics found in a
burial place are the most spectacular
artistic revelation of this period. The
goblet is supposed to have held the
long bones belonging to the dead.
This one is beautifully decorated associating in horizontal bands, a frieze of
wading birds (i.e. herons etc), a frieze
of saluki (Persian greyhounds) and two
exaggeratedly long-horned ibex.

Continue to room 10
then turn right to
room B.

Goblet decorated with animals
Susa c. 4000 BC
Painted terra-cotta – H 29 cm

The Hunting cup
Ugarit, I4th-13th centuries BC
Gold – D 18.8 cm

Sully 4
Floor ground
room B

Retrace your steps
and turn right into
the Sackler wing.

Ugarit, a town on the coast of Syria which developed a palatial civilization at the end of the second millenium BC, characterized by a flowering of luxury crafts in precious and exotic materials found in the houses, tombs, sanctuaries and palaces. Two gold cups were hidden near the Temple of Baal. Today, one is in the Louvre, the other in the Museum of Aleppo in Syria.

The *Hunting Cup* shows a royal hunter on a chariot, shooting with his bow, the chariot reins round his waist. His dog follows him, while game flee in front of the chariot; a goat, a young bull, and a cow accompanied by her calf. An old bull is behind the chariot attacking it with lowered head.

To the ancient East also belong objects from the countries of the Levant. Formerly, the Levant corresponded to the countries bordered by the eastern part of the Mediterranean Ocean, especially Palestine, the Lebanon, Syria, and Anatolia. The smaller kingdoms of the Levant were the link between Mesopotamia and Egypt and later with Mediterranean civilizations. The collections are displayed in rooms A to D and 17 to 21. In room B are exhibited two important pieces from the Phoenician pantheon, coming from Ugarit (Syrian coast): *The Fertility Goddess* carved on the lid of an ivory cosmetics box (late 13th century BC) and the *stele of the storm god Baal* (1350-1250 BC).

19

Capital from a column of the audience chamber (apadana) in the palace of Darius the First at Susa c. 510 BC
Limestone – H 5,80 m

Richelieu 4
Ground floor
rooms 12 a et b

Darius the First (522-486 BC), a Persian noble of the Achemenid clan, seized the Persian throne and took the power of the Empire to its zenith. Susa became the administrative capital of the Empire which stretched from the Mediterranean Ocean to India. He had a gigantic palace built on an artificial terrace measuring 13 hectares (in room 15 you will find information concerning this extraordinary domain).

This monumental capital, the projecting part of which consists of bulls bearing two beams, formerly crowned a column 21 metres high, which was one of thirty six which decorated the audience chamber (apadana). This room, prefiguring that in the Palace of Persepolis, measured 109 metres on one side. The palace was gigantic, worthy of the "king of king" as the king of Persia had himself called.

The palace built by Darius the First included, to the south of the audience chamber, a royal residence with walls decorated by a frieze of glazed bricks. The archers represented here, turned towards the right or the left, but always in the same position, are perhaps guards of the king's household, dressed in court robes (which the king himself wore in time of peace), his dignitaries, and his guardians: an embroidered robe, a twisted headband enclosing their hair. They hold their spear with two hands, their quiver and bow on their shoulder. Other figures also made up the decoration, some of which are to be found here: lions, winged bulls, fabulous animals. Made by casting – which allowed the motifs to be repeated all over the inside walls of the palace –, the siliceous bricks of these panels were then coated with a coloured glazing, which gave them a shiny finish after firing.

The frieze of archers
c. 500 BC
Glazed bricks – H 4.75 m

This handle in the shape of a winged ibex in gold and silver from the Achemenid Persian era (c. 500 BC) shows the persistance of the zoomorphic tradition in the art of metalwork in Iran. It shows the influence of the Orient in the winged, rearing ibex and that of the West in the mask of Silenus at the base of the handle, evidence that Greek creation was conveyed throughout Asia.

In the second millenium BC, the kingdom of Elam consisted of the high valleys of Fars and the plain of Susa. The height of Elamit power was situated at Susa in the 13th and 12th centuries BC. In the 12th century the Elamits overran Babylon and took home to Susa, as loot from the war, masterpieces such as the *Law-Codex of Hammurabi* and the *Stele of Naram-Sin.* The destruction of Susa by the Babylonian king, Nebuchadnezzar I, around 1120 BC, was the beginning of the decline of the Elamits; they had a renaissance in the 8th and 7th centuries but then collapsed after the Assyrians attacked in 646 BC. It was then that the Persians took over the country. Like Elam, the Persian Empire had two capitals: Persepolis and Susa. Cyrus II the Great (c. 559-530 BC) was the founder of the Empire.

Richelieu 4
Ground floor
room 12 a

You will go through several rooms and then go down to the crypt to find the rooms devoted to the Levant. Beyond these rooms, rendezvous room 20.

Achemenid vase handle
c. 5th-4th century BC
Silver and gold – H 0.27 m; W 0.15 m

Richelieu 4
Ground floor
room 20

The department of
Egyptian Antiquities
follows the Oriental
Antiquities.

The trio of Gods
Palmyra,
c. 1st century AD
Limestone – H 60 cm; W 72 cm

Palmyra, a vast oasis in the heart of Syria was a thoroughfare between east and west. It was in a very prosperous position; thanks to its geographical situation, it was at the crossroads of the Greco-Roman world and the Parthian and Sassanid empires. Works coming from Palmyra are exhibited together in room 20. The shrines in Palmyra also received cultic images and altars which proves their devotion to the divinities in a pantheon where Beelshamen, "he whose name is blessed", dominates. *The Trio of Gods* represents the three major divinities of the city, dressed as Roman soldiers: Beelshamen in the middle, on his right the moon-god Aglibol, on his left the sun-god Malakbel.

The granary of Nakhti

Sully 5
Ground floor
room 16

The department of Egyptian antiquities, like that of Oriental Antiquities, displays artistic masterpieces and archeological documents which inform us about the history of these ancient societies.

The Louvre possesses one of the most extensive collections of Egyptian antiquities in the world. They are displayed on two levels: theme-by-theme on the ground floor and chronologically on the first floor, retracing the history of Egyptian art over four thousand years.
For a complete visit of this department, see in the same collection: *Egypt in the Louvre. A guided visit.* (in French)

The visit begins with the theme-by-theme section, on the ground floor.

Archeologists discovered this four thousand year-old model in the tomb of Chancellor Nakhti. Like other objects discovered in the tombs, this granary had a precise function. Indeed, the Egyptians believed that in the next world, the dead had the same needs as in this one. So they put beside them everything that they would find useful. Objects which were too large, such as boats or houses could be represented by miniature models.

These were also used for representing every day activities concerning food: slaughtering of animals, beer-making, ploughing... Granaries were used for storing grain harvests which would be used during the year or put aside for the years of famine, when there was no flooding of the Nile. The earth was fertilized by the limon deposited by annual flooding of the Nile.

Model granary
The tomb of Nakhti
Asyut, c. 1950-1900 BC
Stuccoed and painted wood – H 0.32 m

The coffins of Tamutnefret

Sully 5
Ground floor
room 14

Egyptian civilization was one of the most enduring in the history of mankind (4th millennium BC to the Roman occupation at the beginning of our era). Turned towards the Nile, source of fertility, Egypt quickly developed a centralized political system and a powerful religious faith which gave it extraordinary stability. Because they depended on farming, the Egyptians developed a highly diversified range of crafts to which we owe the records of day-to-day life.

The dead were then carefully embalmed and enveloped in shrouds and linen bandages incorporating protective amulets. The mummy was then "dressed" in cardboard packaging and placed in one or more sarcophagi and put in a stone tank within the tomb. It was only later that animals were sacrificed and mummified like humans.

Egyptian coffins often have the aspect of a human body, here we may see the face, the wig, arms crossed over the breast and the feet. But there also existed simpler ones, large rectangular boxes. As to the number of coffins, this was variable. According to their means, the dead possessed one, two or more. They were encased so as to better protect the body.

Tamutnefret, a singer of Amun was an important woman; able to treat herself to gilt for her face and her hands!

The coffins of Tamutnefret
c. 1200-1100 BC
Painted and gilded wood
H of the outside sarcophagi 1.80 m

The crypt of Osiris

The underground passage where you are now bears the name of one of the great divinities of the Egyptian pantheon: *Osiris*, who was master of the world of the dead and reigned over Abydos, his principal shrine. Recipient of the first rite of mummification, he naturally became the king of the hereafter, having been, beforehand, the king of men.

He may be found wearing a royal crown, bearing royal insignia, sheathed in a shroud, his skin painted black, the colour of the earth, or green the colour of vegetation.

Sully 5
Ground floor
room 13

Statue of Osiris
c. 332-30 BC
Glazed wood and bronze – H 1.58 m

Religion played an important role in the life of the ancient Egyptians. They built temples, for honouring their gods, which are amongst some of the largest monuments left to us by Antiquity. In the Galerie Henri IV, an Egyptian temple has been rebuilt using sometimes monumental remains from different Egyptian shrines.

The very high columns placed at the entrance are among some of the oldest on display here: they date from the time of the pyramids and have elegant palm-leaf capitals.

The colossal statues of pharaohs ornamented the facades and the courtyards of temples as did the vast reliefs of limestone and granite to be seen nearby. At the back of the room, several naos (temples to the gods) come from the most secret part of the temples, the Holy of Holies. They protected, hidden behind doors, the statue of the god in front of which important ceremonies took place.

Sully 6
Ground floor
room 12

Chapel of the god
c. 550 BC
Pink granite – H 2.58 m; W 1.51 m
D 1.50 m

The ancient Egyptians, in the 4th century BC, set up one of the first writing systems of mankind. Whether they are inscribed on papyrus, monuments, or on the wood of sarcophagi, hieroglyphs always seem mysterious.

Each sign drawn by a scribe represents a simple or complex sound, or an idea or a grammatical notion. The signs themselves re-create the everyday Egyptian world. Human beings doing different things, animals, objects tools, may be recognized.

Hieroglyphs possess a sacred and an official character. In every day life Egyptians used different forms of writing, hieratic a simplified script and demotic, more recent, which made its appearance in the first century BC.

It was Champollion, founder of the Egyptian Department of the Louvre, who was the first person to succesfully decipher hieroglyphs in 1822.

Sully 6
Ground floor
room 6

The scribe's equipment:
A palette with red and black ink
c. 1300 BC
Wood – W 37 cm
A cup c. 700-500 BC
China – H 8.8 cm

Papyrus-cutter
bronze – L 24.4 cm
Donation Tyszkiewicz
Beginning of a book of the dead
c. 1000 BC
Papyrus — H 25 cm

A Nile boat

Sully 6
Ground floor
room 3

Egyptian cities were nearly all built along the Nile, along a narrow band of fertile land. Beyond stretched the desert.

The most common means of transport was thus the boat, equipped with oars and sail. The person sitting in the front of the boat held a wooden stick in his hand which allowed him to sound the depth of the river. The annual flooding of the Nile meant it was always navigable. The man sitting at the back steered the boat with two huge oars, following instructions given by the first man.

The miniature model (see also p. 24) was found in a tomb. You can see its owner sitting in the cabin, in the shade, a flower in his hand. This boat necessary for life on earth was probably needed in life after death too.

A Nile boat
c. 1900-1800 BC
Stuccoed and painted wood – L 67 cm

Sully 6
Ground floor
room 4

Go down a few
steps after room 2.

Mastaba of Akhethetep
Detail of a bas-relief:
fishermen
Saqqara, c. 2400 BC
Painted limestone

In Arabic, *mastaba* means bench. Archeologists have chosen this word to designate a type of Egyptian tomb which resembles a huge bench. Here only the chapel remains, the place beneath which the burial vault was hollowed out for the sarcophagi of the dead. They were meant for the important personages of the early history of Egypt and the mastabas were built near to the pharoahs' pyramids.

The chapel remained open so that offerings to the dead could be placed there. The walls were covered with bas-reliefs describing scenes of daily life:

the Egyptians believed that these representations would allow the dead to lead a life in the next world identical to the one they led on earth.

Everything is foreseen for this new life: on the wall on the right hand side, a procession of women bear baskets full of food; on another wall, a hippopotamus hunting scene evokes one of the favorite pastimes of important Egyptian personages; elsewhere a baby goat is born while its mother takes delight in shrub leaves.

The Big Sphinx

This impressive statue with a human head and an animal's body is a sphinx. Guardians of the entrance to Egyptian temples, these strange beings unite the strength of the lion and the intelligence of royalty. Arranged two by two, they mark the path leading to the building. The longest known path which joined the temples of Karnak to those of Luxor had about seven hundred. The Pharoah's face can be recognized by his false beard and his headpiece in striped material, decorated with a serpent on his forehead. This sculpture was found in Tanis, a city situated near the Nile delta.

The granite quarries were at the other end of Egypt. This sphinx weighs roughly 28 tons. The effort accomplished in transporting such a heavy stone with the rudimentary means of the time, must be admired.

Although granite is a very hard stone, difficult to carve, the sculptor was able to create a beautiful stately shape for the body and to stylize the features of the face.

Sully 6
Entresol
The sphynx crypt, room 1

Retrace your steps
Rendez-vous in room 8.

The Big Sphinx
Tanis, c. 1898-1866 BC
Pink granite – H 1.83 m; W 4.80 m

Egyptian furniture

Sully 6
Ground floor
room 8

Showcase of a house
displaying New Kingdom furniture
c. 1550-1069 BC
Wood, wicker-work, pottery

For several decades, thanks to archeology, we have found out more about the setting of the Egyptians' daily life, their palaces and their houses. The custom of taking to the tomb the necessary objects for survival in the next world allowed us to become acquainted with pieces of furniture; they were found in necropolis. Egyptian furniture was made from fragile materials such as wood, sometimes coated in stucco and painted, sometimes inlaid with richer material such as ivory, precious woods, even gold and precious stones.

The shape of furniture has not changed much. Chairs and painted chests, small stools, seem almost contemporary. The beds are different from ours with a head-rest at the top. More common objects, especially the woven baskets, can still be found in the markets.

Go straight ahead, through rooms 9, 10 and ll, and go up the Midi staircase. You are now in the second part of the Egyptian antiquities, displayed in chronological order in rooms 20 to 30. Rendez-vous in room 20.

The Guebel el-Arak Dagger

Sully 6
1st floor
room 20

The Midi staircase was conceived by the architects of Napoléon I, Percier and Fontaine, to lead to the imperial apartments. The Egyptian antiquities collections occupy the rooms which under the Second Empire formed the Sovereigns' Museum.

Pre-dynastic Egypt: the Nagada period (c.4000-3100 BC), when men started to cultivate the banks of the Nile. They deposited potteries full of food for their dead, proving their belief in life after death. They carved ivory and stone vases. The art of bas relief appeared around 3300 BC, on the handles of daggers – such as this one – and on stone palettes. On one side of the handle a battle scene is shown, boats and people tackle each other, in superposed lines.

Dagger from Guebel el-Arak
c. 3200 BC
Blade in silex, handle in ivory
(hippopotamus canine tooth)
H 25.5 cm; handle 4.5 cm

The Seated Scribe

Masterpiece of the Old Kingdom and without doubt the best known Egyptian work of art, *the Scribe* was discovered in a tomb in Saqqara. Thanks to their wide knowledge (writing, mathematics, literature) scribes were higher civil servants in the royal administration.

The personage here is working: sitting cross-legged, a roll of papyrus in his lap he is ready to write. Originally, he was holding a paint brush in his right hand. His paunch indicates that he is well fed, leading an easy, sedentary life.

His flabby body is in opposition to his refined, intelligent face. In order to better express the vivacity of his look, the artist has used inlay technique. The contour of the eyes is in copper, the white of the eye in limpid stone, the iris in rock crystal as transparent as glass.

Sully 6
1st floor
room 22

The "Seated" scribe
Saqqara, c. 2600-2350 BC
Painted limestone, inlaid eyes – H.0.53 cm

Senynefer and Hatchepsout

This sculpture of the New Kingdom, which has kept its beautiful original colours, comes from a tomb. Originally, Hatchepsout and his wife Senynefer were clasping each other in front of a chair back.

Behind what remains, we can see the text of a prayer destined to assure the couple eternal life. The man and woman are carefully dressed and made-up. Both are wearing a wig. The one of Hatchepsout is made of large plaits and decorated with a headband; that of her husband is made of small plaits. Both have their eyes made-up and wear necklaces. Senynefer's is made of gold beads, a reward often given by pharoahs to deserving civil servants.

The two spouses do not have the same coloured skin. In Egypt, tradition had it that women's complexion was suggested by the colour yellow and men's by red ochre. The contrast is accentuated here, but it does correspond to reality. Men were often out of doors, and tanned. Women, in a high social position, on the other hand, stayed indoors at home and protected themselves from the light if they went out. Thus they remained paler.

Sully 6
1st floor
room 24

Senynefer and Hatchepsout
c. 1425-1390 BC
Painted sandstone – H 0.85 m

Portrait of Amenophis IV

This fragment comes from the temple built in Karnak in honour of the sun-god Aton, the only master recognized by Amenophis IV who reigned from 1357 to 1337 BC of the New Kingdom. In honour of Aton, the pharoah even changed his name to Akhenaton, "he who is useful to Aton". The king's features are deliberately distorted (almond shaped eyes, proeminent chin, thick lips) according to the artistic tastes of the time.

In room 26 is reconstituted the Council chamber in the queen's pavilion in the chateau of Vincennes. Room 25 is decorated with panelling which was formerly in the king's bedroom; in the following room have been remounted elements from Henri II's Parade chamber (on the site of the present Seven Fireplaces room, see p. 40), the ceiling of which is by Scibecq de Carpi (1558). Rooms 27 to 30 are those requested by Champollion (1792-1832), who deciphered the hieroglyphs, and the first curator of Egyptian antiquities, under Charles X. The decoration of these rooms, inaugurated in 1827, recall the rediscovery of Egypt.

Sully 6
1st floor
room 25

Fragment of a giant effigy of Amenophis IV-Akheneton
Karnak, c. 1353-1337 BC
Sandstone – H 1.37 m

The "divine worshipper" Karomama

Wishing to draw together the powerful clergy of Amon who had gained control in the region of Thebes, and the royalty governing from the North, the pharoahs of the time instituted one of their daughters "divine worshipper of Amon": wife of the god and his alone, she was invested with vast temporal powers in the region of Thebes. It was Champollion himself who brought this precious statuette to France in 1829 from Egypt. He had been fascinated by its grace. It represents Karomama, a royal princess, "divine worshipper of Amon". Besides being beautiful, this lady presents a wonderful example of inlay work in precious metals in her clothes and jewellery: two large wings envelope her legs; a necklace with a heavy fastener hangs down her back and bears her name, "the beloved of Mout, Karomama".

Sully 6
1st floor
room 29

Parallel to the four rooms where Egyptian works are on show, the Campana rooms extend. You enter through the vestibule, beyond the last room of the Egyptian Antiquities collections. (room 30).

The "divine worshipper"
Karomama
c. 850 BC
Bronze, gold, silver, black and white paste – H 59.5 cm

Sully 6
1st floor
rooms 41, 43 et 44

The collection of Greek vases in the Louvre is one of the finest in the world. Exhibited in the Galerie Campana, which bears the name of a priceless collection of Greek ceramics, acquired by Napoléon III in 1861, it traces the development of shapes, techniques and images.

The "krater (a large bowl for mixing wine and water) of Eurytios" illustrates a minor episode from the life of Hercules: the hero won the archery competition organised by King Eurytios and thus obtained the king's daughter's hand. However, a question arose after the victory and Hercules killed one of the king's sons, Iphitos. The episode is recounted in a banquet scene, uniting the protagonists whose names are inscribed in characters from the Corinthian alphabet.

The Etruscan aristocracy (the krater was found in Cerveteri in Etruria) prized this kind of bowl produced in Corinth. This one is exceptional in its large size and careful decoration: black figures with red highlights stand out against a light backdrop. These colours are obtained by chemical reactions in the clay after several firings.

Krater with black figures
called *"the Eurytios krater"*
c. 600 BC
Terracotta – H 46 cm – E635
Room 41, showcase 13

Heracles and Cerberus (side A)
Amphora attributed to the potter
Andokides found in Etruria
c. 530-520 BC
Terracotta – H 59.5 cm – F 204
Room 43, showcase 21

Amphora from Attica with red figures
called the *"Melos or Milo amphora"*
Attributed to the Painter of Suessula.
c. 410-400 BC
Terracotta – H 69.5 cm – MNB 810
Room 44, showcase 21

Hercules and Cerberus

The Melos or Milo Amphora

This amphora was made c. 530 BC by the potter Andokides who elaborated the red figure technique in Athens. The silhouettes are detailed in a more refined way. The red figure appeared towards 530 BC and confirmed the superiority of the workshops in Athens. On this amphora, Hercules is shown accomplishing the twelfth task, the most perilous of them all: the capture of Cerberus, the abominable three-headed dog, guardian of hell. After defeating the beast he delivered Theseus from the world of the dead.

The abundant decoration on the "Milo Amphora" reminds us of the graphically audacious Parthenon sculptures supervised by the master Phidias (see p. 50). The painter uses the shape of the amphora to suit his purpose of placing numerous faces of gods on it. In the middle we see Zeus getting ready to strike a giant seen from behind. Near to him, the winged victory shoots forward on his chariot; at his feet, Hercules bends his bow, whilst Athena shoots forward in the foreground, killing an enemy on the ground. All around, the Olympians, Aries and Aphrodite, Apollo and Artemis, Poseidon ... lead a victorious battle against their enemies.

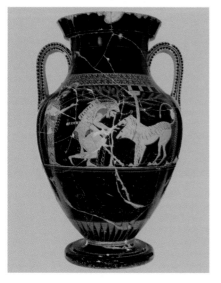

Louis XIV first of all had the Galerie Henri IV refitted (a fire had destroyed it in 1661) and decorated by Charles Le Brun who chose Apollo the sun-god as his subject since the king liked to be identified with him. The décor was only finished two centuries later by Eugène Delacroix, who painted the motif in the centre of the ceiling, showing Apollo defeating the serpent Python.

In the last display case in the middle of the gallery are exhibited the few remaining crown jewels. An enormous 140 carat diamond, the *Regent*, was bought by Philippe d'Orléans, regent of France, who governed the kingdom until Louis XV became of age. The large pink ruby, cut in the shape of a dragon, is called the *Cote de Bretagne* and belonged to Anne de Bretagne; the ruby then passed to her daughter, wife of Francis I. The *Sancy* owned by the Chancellor of the Exchequer of Henri IV, weighs 54 carats.

Continue straight ahead. The kings from Henri II to Louis XIV lived in this part of the palace. chambers, closets, antechambers and state gallery. The king's bedroom, the Henri II antechamber (room 38), on the right, a composition by Braque, *Les Oiseaux* (I953) has replaced the ceiling by Scibecq de Carpi (see p. 36): then comes the guardroom (room 32). In the king's Grand Cabinet antique glassware is displayed (room 34); the Apollo rotunda precedes the gallery of the same name.

Richelieu
1st floor
room 66

Continue westwards. You are now near to the *Victoire de Samothrace* ...

Eugène Delacroix (1798-1863)
Apollo defeating the serpent Python, detail from the ceiling decoration

Louis XV's crown
Paris, 1722
Gilded silver

The *Victoire de Samothrace* dominates with its great stature, the stately staircase which has replaced the one built at the beginning of the nineteenth century by the architects Percier and Fontaine. Go down the staircase. It is preferable to admire the *Victoire* from below – originally it was situated on a rocky terrace overhanging the sea.

Among all the original Greek works known, it is one of the most important masterpieces of Hellenistic sculpture (323-31 BC, see p. 51). It was in pieces when found in 1863 by a French archeologist in Samothraki, an island in the Aegean sea.

This work, which commemorates a Rhodian naval victory (towards 190 BC), is doubtless, together with the *Mona Lisa,* the most famous in the Louvre.

Its place, at the top of the staircase, since 1883, renders it even more impressive and gives it a magnificent appearance: its wings spread, left leg in front, tunic flattened by the spray, but rising into waves behind because of the wind. We can almost hear the wind blowing through the tunic. If we judge by the beauty of the work, the artist who did the sculpture must have been famous, but his name remains unknown to us.

Victory of Samothrace
Samothrace, c. 190 BC
Marble – H 3.28 m

Denon
1st floor
on the landing

Go down the stairs to the ground floor and walk through the Daru gallery.

The Borghese Gladiator

Denon
Ground floor
room B galerie Daru

In the galerie Daru works evoking the origins of the collections of Greek, Etruscan and Roman antiquities are displayed.

Bought by Napoléon I from his brother-in-law, the Prince Borghese in 1808 together with the rest of his collection, the *Borghese Gladiator* was much imitated and admired during the seventeenth and eighteenth centuries. He appears to be a warrior rather than a gladiator since he has a shield strapped to his left arm. Perhaps he belonged to a group or was associated with another warrior?

Showing proof of his mastery of his art, the sculptor has rendered the muscles of his model perfectly, almost turning him into anatomical model. The work may be admired from all angles. In the middle of the Hellenistic period, (see p. 51) this work illustrates the values of the classical period (see p. 50). Agasias of Ephesus who signed the trunk of the original, worked in Asia Minor and exported his work to Italy.

The new conquerors of the Greek kingdoms, the Romans showed themselves to be great lovers of copies of Greek art.

At the end of the galerie Daru, turn left in the *Salle du Manège* where the Prince Imperial, son of Napoléon III took his riding lessons. In this room with its capitals decorated with animals, sculptures consisting of antique and more recent elements are exhibited.

Take the escalator down to the entresol, to the right of which are the old stables of Napoléon III, the pre-classical Greek gallery, and the beginning of the tour of the collection of Greek antiquities.

A warrior called
the *"Borghese Gladiator"*
c. 100 BC
Marble – H 1.57 m

Cycladic woman's head

Denon 8
Entresol
room 1

The chronological tour begins in the pre-classical Greece gallery where the pre-Hellenic Cycladic civilizations are evoked together with Minoan Crete and the Mycenean civilizations whose creations illustrate the birth of Greek art.

Greek civilization developed from the 16th century BC. Through the centuries art has advanced considerably. Three principal periods can be distinguished:
– The archaic period (6th century BC),
– Classical Greece (5th – 4th centuries BC),
– The Hellenistic period (3rd – 1st centuries BC).
A knowledge of Greek art is necessary in order to appreciate Roman art which found its source there, but also to understand all the creators of the following centuries, who during the Middle Ages, the Renaissance and modern times (classical for example) tried to find once again, an ideal beauty created two thousand years earlier in Greece.

This head belongs to the family of figures and statuettes that artists of the Cyclades created during the ancient bronze age (3200-200 BC). She probably belonged to the known diagram of a nude statue of a woman, arms crossed over the breasts, and measuring about 1.50 m. It is one of the first pieces of evidence of Greek sculpture in marble; its modernity struck sculptors, such as Brancusi at the beginning of our century.

We do not know her identity but her religious character seems likely.

Woman's head
Cycladic art, c. 2700-2400 BC
Marble – H 27 cm; W 14.5 cm

44

This small statue was found in the storerooms of the Museum of Auxerre (Burgundy). Her origin is unknown, but her style and the material she is made from, soft limestone, relates her to 7th century BC Cretan art. The design engraved on her dress must have been brightened with colours, traces of which still remain. She is in an attitude of worship, her body corseted in a narrow dress her right hand raised to her breast, the left along the side of her body, illustrating the Daedalian style, from the name of the mythical engineer, Daedal to whom antique tradition attributes the invention of the art of statuary. Other characteristics are: the U-shaped face sketching a smile, the heavy layered hair.

Dame d'Auxerre
Crete? c. 630 BC
Limestone – H 75 cm (base included)

Characteristic of Archaic Greece, this statue was discovered on the Greek island of Samos in the shrine of Hera. On the side seam of her dress we can see an inscription which reads: "Cheramyes has dedicated me to Hera as an offering". She is a kore, an image of a woman in all her splendour, offered to the god – the male equivalent is called a *Kouros*, a nude male of athletic build.

The arms of the kore are flat along her body and her feet held tightly together She wears ceremonial dress: a long refined pleated linen skirt *chitra* over this is draped a largely pleated shawl of wool *himation*. Unforunately her head is missing.

From 900 BC onwards, Greek civilization developed around the Mediterranean basin. The period stretching from 620 to 480 BC is called Archaic and is marked by the first building in stone of temples and the emergence of marble statues representing figures in a conventional and rather rigid manner.

Denon 8
Entresol
room 1

The Kore of Samos
Samos, *c. 570-580 BC*
Marble – H 1.92 m

The head
of the Rampin horseman

Head of the Rampin horseman
c. 550 BC
Marble – H 0.27 m

Denon 8
Entresol
room 1

This sculpture owes its name to George Rampin, the collector who made a gift of it to the Louvre in 1896. It was found on the Acropolis in Athens.

The head is authentic, whilst the body is a casting, the original being in Athens. The face is lightened by a soft smile, typical of archaic art. The sculptor has taken particular care with the curls of the beard, which are figured as very fine "pearls"; to make the beard appear really thick, small pearls have been inserted between the larger ones. The same technique has been used for the hair. Originally the sculpture was painted and even now we can see small traces of colour: black for the eyes and moustache, red in the beard and hair. The head is crowned with leaves. Is it perhaps the crown of victory? On the Acropolis, the remains of a second horseman have been found. Without being absolutely sure, it is thought that perhaps there were two heroes, Castor and Pollux or Hippias and Hipparque, sons of Pisistratus, tyrant of Athens.

The Louvre's collection of Greek, Etruscan and Roman antiquities came from the former French royal collection, enriched by those of Cardinals Richelieu and Mazarin. The section was created in 1795. Acquisitions and bequests later enlarged it considerably.

During the first Empire (amongst others) Napoléon I bought an important collection from his brother-in-law, the Prince of Borghese; then throughout the 19th and 20th centuries various other pieces or collections were either bought or bequeathed in wills.

This krater signed by Euphronios, the most famous painter of the late 6th century BC, is representative of the golden age of painting using the red figure technique. The scene describes the struggle between Hercules and the giant Antaeus. The Greek hero with his expressionless face and crown of black curls, is destroying the body of his enemy, whose face is haggard, his beard unkempt, his eyes revulsed and his mouth hanging open announcing his coming death. Antaeus, a dangerous giant, compelled passers-by to wrestle with him, killing all those he defeated. He built a temple using the skulls of his victims for the roof. As long as he touched the ground he was invincible. Hercules lifted him off the ground, and holding him up in the air, strangled him.

Chalice shaped krater with red figures Signed by Euphronios, a painter from Atticus, c. 510 BC
Terracotta – H 48 cm

Denon 8
Entresol
room 1

At the end of the gallery, in the room where works illustrating the Severe style period, including the famous *Miletus Torso* (c. 480 BC), turn right to go to the rooms devoted to Egyptian Christian art: that of the Copts.

Denon 8
Entresol
room 2

Christianity developed very early in Egypt, from the first centuries of our era. The name given to Christians of the Nile valley is Coptic, their art takes its inspiration from pharaonic, classical and Christian traditions. The "Coptic art gallery" displays its development both chronologically and theme by theme. Egypt is a land of hermitages and monasteries. Baouit is important evidence. The monastery was founded at the end of the fourth century, and was dedicated to Saint Apollo. The south church, reconstituted in the "Baouit room", dates from the end of the sixth century. It contains beautifully sculpted decors in wood and limestone and an important series of capitals.
In relation with the church, sculptures and paintings from the monasteries are exhibited.
A large display case contains complete outfits of clothing and a glimpse of weaving techniques which constitute a major aspect of Coptic art.

One of the facades of the Baouit monastery reconstituted.

Turn back on your steps to continue the tour of the Greek, Etruscan and Roman antiquities. After the *Milet Torso,* go up a few stairs and you will find yourself in the room where remains of the sculpted decor of the temple of Zeus in Olympia are displayed. Go out on the left, then turn right and go straight ahead to room 7.

This work dates from the 5th century BC, the zenith of Greek civilization in intellectual and artistic domains. It is the "classical" era. Athens becomes a "beacon" town. On the Acropolis (the city on the hill), Pericles has an immense temple built and dedicated to the goddess Athena, the Parthenon.

The plaque in the Louvre is only a fragment of a frieze measuring 160 metres which adorned the Parthenon's peristyle gallery, associating about 360 people commemorating, the great Panathenaic feast: every four years the Athenians went to the Acropolis to offer to Athena the tutelary goddess of the city, a tunic woven by young girls from the best families and called Ergastines. We see them here, with two men, the organizers of the ceremony. The slow and solemn march of the procession is suggested by the hang of their clothes (peplos). Gracefulness and sobriety harmonize in this masterpiece of classical art.

In the classical era, artists were more concerned with reality when reproducing the human body. The figures are no longer stiff as in the archaic era; they now move in space, are well proportioned and give an impression of balance and calm, the ideal of classical beauty.

Sully 7
Ground floor
room 7

Go through the long gallery at the end of which you will find the tall figure of Melpomene. In the last room there are Roman copies of original Greek works by the sculptor Praxiteles.
Turn left and you will reach, from behind, one of the masterpieces of the Louvre museum.

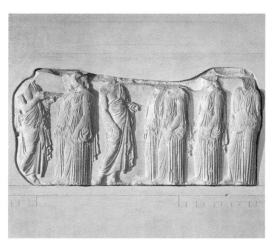

Plaque called the Ergastines
Parthenon, Panathenaic frieze
445-438 BC
Marble – H 96 cm; W 2.07 m

Aphrodite called the Venus of Milo
Melos, c. 100 BC
Marble – H 2.02 m

After the conquests of Alexander (334-323 BC) Greek civilization radiated over an immense area. According to the areas, works of art may be very different. Let us remember, mainly, some new elements: movement in sculpture was more and more accentuated, and as here; a marked preference for describing extremes – childhood, old age, ugliness, suffering – to the detriment of the ideal of calm and balance valued by the classical era.

Sully 7
Ground floor
room 12

Go straight ahead, turn right into the salle des Caryatides. (room 17).

Known all over the world, this statue was found in the Greek island of Melos (or Milo) in 1820. Venus being her Roman name and Aphrodite her name in Greek, she is the goddess of love. Observe the realism of the bust which seems to emerge from the heavy folds of the garment. The position of the left leg gives the impression of a body in motion as does the torsion of the bust. Going round the sculpture, we can better understand all the subtlety of its position in space. The serene beauty of the *Venus de Milo* confirms that Hellenistic artists were sometimes inspired by works of the classical era.

The salle des Caryatides and the Henri II staircase

The most beautiful room in the Louvre, the Salle des Caryatides, was designed by the architect Pierre Lescot for the king, Henri II (1547-1559), then later transformed.

The original room, with exposed beams, was vaulted in the seventeenth century, then totally redecorated by Percier and Fontaine when it was definitely assigned to antique sculptures of the museum.

Jean Goujon, a sixteenth century sculptor, is the author of the statues of women, called caryatides which uphold the gallery.

Four royal weddings were the opportunities for holding memorable feasts here. The body of Henri IV, who was assassinated by Ravaillac, laid in state here. Molière acted here four times between 1658 and 1664. This area became, at the Revolution in 1692, the "salle des Antiques", where the royal collections of antique and modern sculptures and plaster casts were exhibited.

The Henri II staircase, the oldest staircase in the Louvre, following this room also dates from the middle of the sixteenth century. It leads to the large guardroom on the first floor and the royal apartments. During important ceremonies, Swiss guards were placed on each stair. On the ground floor landing the person in charge of tasting the dishes to be served to the king would sit. This staircase with its straight banisters and its cradle shaped vault, decorated with a panelled ceiling is typical of French Renaissance art. The reliefs of the vault illustrate hunting scenes, executed by Jean Goujon's workshop, associated with the king's monogram.

Marsyas awaiting torture

The Salle des Caryatides houses Roman sculpture, replicas of Greek works from the Hellenistic era. Many Greek statues were in bronze. Most of them have disappeared, the metal being used for other purposes (arms, plates and dishes).

The Hellenistic sculptors liked picturesque scenes – a child playing with a goose, another on the back of a centaur. They often expressed violent feelings, thus the fear of this personage hanging from a tree. The satyr Marsyas, defeated in a music contest was sufficiently audacious to defy the god Apollo and was condemned to be skinned alive. Hanging by his wrists from a tree, he is already suffering; his muscles bulging and painful. The realism of this representation is characteristic of Hellenistic style.

Sully 7
Ground floor
room 17

Return to the Olympia room under the staircase leading to the *Victoire de Samothrace.*
Go through this room, on the opposite side, and you will find yourself in the Etruscan art collection.

Marsyas awaiting torture
Roman replica
of a Greek model from
the School of Pergame,
c. late 3rd century BC
Marble – H 2.56 m

The Sarcophagus
of a married couple

This sarcophagus shows, on its lid, a dead couple of Etruscan nobility. They are shown half-reclining, according to the traditional attitude at banquets. The woman wears a round Etruscan bonnet and boots with curved toes. The lower part of the body appears passive, the bust on the contrary is full of expression, the face smiling. The artist has found how to translate the bond of affection between the couple: the husband has his arm round his wife's shoulders.

Etruscan civilization blossomed in central Italy (Tuscany and Latium). At its zenith (6th century BC) it extended as far as Campania and the plain of the river Po. Etruscan cities flourished progressively according to the Greek model from the end of the 8th century BC, but arts and crafts, which provide evidence from this era of the intensification of exchanges with the Mediterranean and contacts with the Greek world, have reached us especially through discoveries made in tombs. Most of the Etruscan oblects displayed in this museum come from tombs.

Denon 8
Ground floor
room 18

Now turn right after the sarcophagus and enter the appartments of Anne of Austria.

*Sarcophagus
of a married couple*
Caere, c. 530-510 BC
Terracota – H 1.14 m; L 1.90 m

The Portrait of Livia

Portrait of Livia
c. 30 BC
Basalt – H 0.34 m

Denon 8
Ground floor
room 24

Livia was the wife of Emperor
Augustus – 27 BC-14 AD. At the time
of this portrait she was about 30, with a
hair style fashionable at the beginning of
the Roman Empire: a knot of hair over
her forehead, a small bun at the back of
her neck, and a small plait at the top of
her head. The material used, basalt, is
quite unusual. This stone, difficult to
carve, gives her face an almost metallic
appearance. The features are firm with a
solemn, rather distant expression, as if to
idealize the personage.

On the ground floor of the
"Petite Galerie", built under
Henri IV, the architect Louis le
Vau designed between 1655
and 1658 a suite of six rooms
intended as the summer
apartment of Queen Anne of
Austria, mother of Louis XIV.
Today they house Roman
sculpture. The decoration was
done by the Italian painter
Romanelli and the sculptor
Michel Anguier did the stucco
work. Notice especially, on
the left, the Seasons drawing
room (salon des Saisons).
The Queen's apartments were
only open to the public in the
eighteenth century, after the
departure of the court to
Versailles. Ancient sculptures
from Italy were housed there
under Napoléon I.

Rendez-vous in the
large courtyard with
the mosaic floor.

Denon 8
Ground floor
room 30

*Mosaic pavement
of a reception room
in the "Constantine villa'
at Daphne (a suburb of
Antioch in Turkey), c. 325 AD
L 8.07 m; W 8.04 m*

This vast mosaic, measuring more than 8 metres on one side, decorated the floor of a villa situated at Daphne, near Antioche-sur-Oronte, one of the most important cities of the Roman Empire. The richness of this flooring gives an idea of the richness of the villa. In the corners, the busts of four women symbolize virtues. All around twelve small rectangular panels represent subject pictures: shepherds with their flock, florists making garlands, angels banqueting. Four large female figures placed in the corners symbolize the seasons. Between these figures four large trapezoidal panels represent hunting scenes: Meleagre and Atalanta struggling with a terrible boar, huntsmen attacking bears, lions and tigers. This is one of the biggest mosaics known from antiquity.

Roman art was greatly influenced by the prestigious creations of Ancient Greece and flourished especially from the 3rd century BC onwards. As a manifestation of political power many public monuments were built, often decorated with a bas relief recalling a battle or a victory. Art was also used as a social instrument: portraiture was the principal domain where this thirst for recognization was expressed. More and more important people wanted their likeness sculpted. The decoration of private villas and public places benefitted from the art of mosaic, of which the Louvre has some fine examples.

Go across the courtyard, enter on the right, into another room where mosaics are displayed. Go up the Victoire de Samothrace staircase. At the top, rendez-vous on the right in the Percier and Fontaine rooms.

Rooms of the musée Napoléon

Napoléon I commissioned a grand staircase from the architects Percier and Fontaine which gave admittance to the rooms where paintings were exhibited in the Museum. At the request of Napoléon III, who found the staircase too unpretentious, the architect Lefuel destroyed it in 1855: today only the landing remains, consisting of the Percier and Fontaine rooms (named after the two architects).

The new staircase remained unfinished at the fall of the Empire (1870). Work started on it again in 1883; the *Victoire de Samothrace* discovered 20 years earlier was placed there. It only acquired its present appearance in the 1930s.

The Salon carré housed, until 1914, all the chefs d'oeuvres of all periods. It was here that were held regularly, from the end of the seventeenth century, exhibitions of living artists. In 1810 the wedding of Napoléon the Ist and Marie-Louise of Austria, was celebrated here...

The Grande Galerie comes after the Salon carré. These two rooms were the only spaces in the museum when it was opened in 1793. La Grande Galerie (450 m) was built by Henri IV and connected the Louvre to the Tuileries Palace that Catherine de Médicis had built in 1564. It was the place where royal receptions were held. It was here too that the king laid his hands on the sick on the day of his coronation. It is said that the future Louis XIII amused himself here during the camel races and fox hunting organized by his father, Henri IV.
Now, in these two places, the heart of the palace, works of Italian painting, "the core" of the Louvre collections are displayed, most of them from the royal collections of Francis I and Louis XIV.

Auguste Couder (1789-1873)
Napoléon visiting the Louvre under the escort of the architects Percier and Fontaine
1833
Canvas – H 1.775 m; W 1.35 m

Denon 8
1st floor
rooms 1, 2, 3, 5

The paintings of the Middle Ages were mainly displayed in churches and monasteries. They portrayed religious subjects intended to honour God, Jesus, the Virgin and the saints. During the Byzantine era, painters painted scenes that would provide a focus for prayer: they were not seeking to imitate reality, but to convey the grandeur and majesty of God and the saints. Accurate representation of human figures was not considered important. The background of such paintings would be covered with gold, which was seen as the colour of divinity.

Cimabue, a Florentine painter, used a less austere style than Byzantine artists. He introduced new features to painting: in this picture the colours of the figures' clothes are transparent, while those of the angels' wings gradually recede into shade. He also creates an impression of depth by placing the angels carefully and by artful depiction of the dimensions of the throne. Cimabue greatly influenced the art of Giotto.

The first works displayed in the collection of Italian paintings are those of the "Primitive" painters, such as Cimabue and Giotto. Their work was rediscovered at the end of the eighteenth century.

Denon 8
1st floor
room 3 Salon carré

Cenni di Pepe
known as **Cimabue** (c. 1240 - c. 1302)
Virgin and Child in majesty surrounded by six angels
Wood – H 4.27 m; W 2.80 m

Saint Francis of Assisi receiving the stigmata

A painting on wood or a work of sculpture placed above a church altar is known as an altarpiece.

In this work Giotto describes four episodes from the life of Saint Francis of Assisi who abandoned the material world in order to live as Christ had done, in poverty and simplicity. Painted thirty years after the time of Cimabue, Giotto's picture shows a radical development in the art of portraying the human figure. In the large central panel, Saint Francis is shown kneeling, his hands, feet and heart pierced by rays emanating from Christ, depicted as an angel with six wings: he is receiving the stigmata, the marks of the wounds suffered by Christ during the Passion. Giotto was an innovator, introducing a new method of painting which made a great impression on his contemporaries. He was one of the first artists to create an impression of the real world: Saint Francis is shown here as an ordinary man with a landscape of rocks and a few trees.

Denon 8
1st floor
room 3 Salon carré

Giotto di Bondone (c. 1265-1337)
Saint Francis of Assisi receiving the stigmata about 1300
Wood – H 3.13 m; W 1.63 m

59

Denon 8
1st floor
room 3 Salon carré

At the near end of
the *Grande Galerie*,
turn right into the
*salle des Sept-
Mètres*.

This painting commemorates the Florentine victory over the Sienese armies in June 1432. The other two panels of the work are on display separately in Florence and London. The painting should be looked at from right to left, which is the direction of the movement it conveys. The horse on the right side of the painting is at rest, while the white one next to it is preparing to move, the black one is beginning to move, and the brown one towards the left is in full flow. It is as if a single movement has been broken down into its component parts, like that of the lances which slope down in the shape of a fan from right to left. The Florentine captain, in the centre of the painting, gives the signal to attack.

Paolo di Dono
known as **Paolo Uccello** (1397-1475)
*The Battle of San Romano:
the counter-attack of Micheletto
da Cotignola* about 1435
Wood – H 1.82 m; W 3.17 m

Uccello became famous in his time for his attempts to represent the third dimension (perspective). In this work, depth is suggested by the placement of the horses and soldiers lined up in front of each other. We can only see one horse clearly, but we can see many horses' legs; similarly, we can only see one soldier, but we can see many weapons.

Portrait of a young princess of Esta

Named after its dimensions, the *salle des Sept-Mètres* (Seven-metre room), illuminated by a large window, contains fifteenth-century paintings from Siena and Northern Italy. The princely courts of Northern Italy, away from the aesthetic revolution taking place in Florence, preferred a more traditional, refined style, influenced by the gothic era. Pisanello became a favourite of the princes early in his career and he produced many portraits of them on medals, in profile.

In his portrait of a princess of the Esta family (possibly princess Lucia), he successfully achieved an accurate likeness while at the same time incorporating a number of the symbolic features beloved of his contemporaries. The young girl is pictured against a background of butterflies and flowers. On her shoulder she wears an olive branch, symbol of peace and happiness. On her sleeve a double-handled vase represents the coat of arms of the Esta family. Pisanello, although he was gifted in the art of perspective, preferred to show the Princess in profile, as if she were appearing on a piece of ancient money.

Antonio Puccio, known as **Pisanello** (c. 1395-1455)
Portrait of a young princess of Esta
Wood – H 0.43 m; W 0.30 m

Denon 8
1st floor
room 4

Return to the *Grande Galerie.*

61

The Crucifixion

Andrea Mantegna
(c. 1431-1506)
The Crucifixion
about 1456-1459
Wood – H 0.76 m; W 0.96 m

This work was originally part of an altarpiece consisting of six sections, commissioned from the Italian painter Mantegna to decorate St. Zeno's Church in Verona. During the revolutionary period, it was stolen by the French occupying forces, dismembered and taken to France. It is now scattered in three different places: the basilica of St. Zeno, to which the *Virgin and Child with Saints* has been returned; the Louvre, which has kept the Crucifixion, and the Museum of Tours, which contains the two other panels of the lower section of the altarpiece (predella), the *Agony in the Garden* and the *Resurrection.* In order to emphasise the drama of Calvary, Mantegna, who was at this time at the height of his powers, set about an ambitious recreation of classical antiquity. He created a barren, desolate Golgotha in which his skill in conveying depth, space and volume could fully express itself.

Mantegna was particularly interested in Ancient Greece and Rome and spent much of his working life experimenting with perspective.

Portrait of an old man and a young boy

This elderly man belongs to that class of the bourgeoisie, bankers and merchants, which made Florence into one of the richest cities of fifteenth-century Europe. They provided patronage for artists and commissioned work from them for their homes and churches. They would also commission portraits of themselves, as this old man did from Ghirlandaio, unless, as is generally believed, this portrait was painted after the man's death, in honour of his memory.

The man's face, with its pronounced wrinkles, hollow cheeks and warts on the nose, is lacking in charm, but his expression is touching nevertheless; it is a pleasure to behold because we are moved by the tenderness with which he contemplates the child. Ghirlandaio was a greatly respected artist; like the Flemish painters particularly admired by Florentine artists of the fifteenth century, he was a great draughtsman and could paint in great detail – as shown here by the expert precision with which he has painted the old man's white hair and the hairs of the fur.

The east wing of the Grande Galerie contains Italian paintings from the fifteenth and early sixteenth centuries.

Denon 8
1st floor
room 5

Domenico Ghirlandaio (1449-1494)
Portrait of an old man and a young boy about 1490
Wood – H 0.63 m; W 0.46 m

Raphaël, one of the greatest Italian painters to have worked both in Florence and in Rome, painted this picture of the Virgin Mary, baby Jesus and St. John the Baptist in a rural setting at the beginning of his career. The way in which the other two figures gaze at Jesus shows the affection in which they hold him; a single curving line seems to bind them all together. The atmosphere created is a peaceful one. All seems simple, natural and relaxed. However, the presence of the ancolia flower and of dandelion allude to Christ's Passion; Saint John the Baptist's cross is that of the Sacrifice, and the book which the Virgin is giving to Jesus is the one in which his destiny is written. The man nicknamed "the divine Raphaël" was a great painter of the Renaissance; the numerous Madonnas he painted firmly established his reputation and inspired many later artists, especially those of the nineteenth century.

Raffaello Santi
known as **Raphaël,** (1483-1520)
The Virgin and Child with the young Saint John the Baptist, known as *The Beautiful Gardener* 1507
Poplar – H 1.22 m; W 0.80 m

Denon 8
1st floor
room 5

The Sermon of Saint Stephen

Denon 8
1st floor
room 5

Vittore Carpaccio,
(c. 1472 - c. 1525)
The Sermon of Saint Stephen at Jerusalem
about 1514
Canvas – H 1.48 m; W 1.94 m

Saint Stephen, standing on the pedestal of a ruined ancient statue, preaches the Gospel against the backdrop of an idealized vision of Jerusalem. In Venice at the beginning of the sixteenth century, the *scuole,* religious brotherhoods created by local artisans, commissioned paintings of scenes from the lives of their patron saints to decorate their assembly halls. Those of the Scuola di Santo Stefano asked Carpaccio, the most distinctive of all the painters living in Venice at the time, to paint a series of five panels narrating the life of Saint Stephen. *The Sermon* is the second of these panels. The saint is shown addressing an audience in varied costumes which symbolize different parts of the world, thus showing that the Bible's message is relevant to all peoples.

Carpaccio created a highly original style of narrative painting in which every single element of the composition, itself highly structured, contributed towards understanding the scene portrayed. The regular contours of the architecture, the huge, airy spaces and the broad expanses of light all contribute together to an impression of calm, while the artist's use of rich and luminous colours provide the scene with a touch of the exotic.

The Death of the Virgin

Denon 9
1st floor
room 7

Michelangelo Merisi
known as **Caravaggio** (1571-1610)
The Death of the Virgin about 1605-6
Canvas – H 3.69 m; W 2.45 m

Nothing in this image of a woman lying on a bed identifies it as a religious scene, apart from the halo above the woman's head. It is nevertheless true that she is the Virgin Mary, surrounded by the apostles and Mary Magdalene. The artist has deliberately given a human dimension to these sacred figures. Their appearance in this work is quite unusual for a religious painting. With this innovation, Caravaggio, a grand master who spent the best part of his career in Rome at the turn of the sixteenth and seventeenth centuries, began a complete revolution. He also introduced the use of darkness as a dominant feature of his compositions to emphasise colour and provide contrast to light.

The light in this picture brightly illuminates Mary Magdalene, crouched in the foreground, the face of the dead woman and the heads of the apostles. Legend has it that the artist met the woman he eventually used as a model for the Virgin by chance in the street. Commissioned by a convent, this painting caused a huge scandal. This did not prevent Caravaggio's technique from influencing many painters, particularly in France, throughout the seventeenth century.

Virgin with a rabbit

Denon 9
1st floor
room 6

To view the Virgin with a Rabbit, retrace your steps. In the middle of the Grande Galerie is the entrance to the salle des Etats (room 6), where parliament met in the time of Napoléon III.

Tiziano Vecellio
known as **Titian**
(1488/1489-1576)
Virgin with a rabbit
about 1530
Canvas, H 0.71 m; W 0.87 m

This is a touching picture in which a young mother shows a small rabbit to her baby. To her right, a shepherd is resting. A basket of fruit filled with apples and grapes lies at the feet of the Virgin. A glorious twilight sky, crossed with rays of orange and blue, and the use of colours which seem to melt into each other establish the prevailing atmosphere; the composition is luminous and elegant. It conveys a strong impression of serenity and a sense of poetry.

The significance given to landscape was a new departure in Renaissance painting. Titian, the greatest Venetian painter of the sixteenth century, was one of those responsible for this development. At the time when Federico II Gonzaga, who is included in the picture in the features of the shepherd, commissioned this devotional work from Titian, the artist was the most respected in Venice. He made an enormous contribution towards making the Renaissance a period of such richness and creativity.

Mona Lisa

Denon 9
1st floor
room 6

Leonardo da Vinci, (1452-1519)
The Joconda, portrait of Mona Lisa
1503-1507
Wood – H 0.77 m; W 0.53 m

She has provoked fascination and fantasy for centuries; yet can anyone explain exactly why she is so famous? Leonardo da Vinci was not only a painter but also a sculptor, an architect, a musician, a philosopher and an engineer; four centuries before our time, he invented a flying machine. Francis I invited him to come to France and work for him at Fontainebleau.

The identity of the model remained unknown for many years. She is now thought to have been Lisa Gherardini, daughter of a rich family of merchants, who married Francesco del Giocondon in 1495. She is seated on a balcony overlooking an extensive and eerie landscape; strangely-shaped rocks can be seen through a bluish mist.

When Leonardo began his portrait, the young woman was in mourning for her baby daughter; this is why she wears a black veil over her head. To lift her spirits, Leonardo brought musicians and clowns into his studio. Their antics brought a smile to her lips, a smile of undefinable sadness and great gentleness, which made the portrait famous. If viewed for a long period of time, her expression seems to change. Her features seem alive and moving. To make her so astonishingly lifelike, Leonardo used a technique called *sfumato* which consists of obscuring the contours of the painting, to create the impression of a gentle progression from darkness to light. The artist spent many years painting this portrait, reworking it endlessly to achieve the degree of perfection he desired. He was never parted from it, and took it with him on all his travels. It is thought that Francis I purchased it from Leonardo's heirs, many years after the death of the artist.

Denon 9
1st floor
room 6

The largest painting in the Louvre – it measures sixty-seven square metres – was commissioned from Veronese by the monks of the abbey of San Giorgio Maggiore in Venice to decorate a wall of their monastery dining hall.

The subject for the painting chosen by the monks was Christ's first miracle, which took place during a wedding banquet at Cana in Galilee. Veronese decided to portray the precise moment the miracle happened. The servants, pouring the liquid from the jars, notice that it is no longer water, but wine, while the magnificently dressed character, near the centre of the painting, is tasting the new drink. Veronese has placed this episode from the New Testament in architectural surroundings which resemble sixteenth-century Venice and included one hundred and thirty human figures. The atmosphere thus created is more that of a Renaissance banquet than that of a wedding feast of the Ancient World. The married couple, clothed in sumptuous Renaissance garments, are consigned to the left hand end of the table while Christ, his mother and the apostles, wearing only the simple clothes of Ancient times, take centre stage. On their right we may see prelates of the Church. The scene is enlivened by servants, clowns, dwarves and animals such as a parrot, a small spaniel who has climbed onto the table, and some greyhounds. On the left, a steward tells the married couple of the miracle.

Important restoration work carried out between 1990 and 1992 allowed the colours in this painting to be completely renewed. The artist was able to use the finest quality pigments. Lapis lazuli, used to create the colour blue, was the most precious of these. The achievement of the artist was to use only a small number of colours to create a symphonic effect which conveys all the magnificence of the feast.

The scene was designed to convey Christ's message. A young woman on the right throws eglantine, symbols of Christ's Passion and of the Virgin Mary, from a balcony. The meat, probably lamb, hints at the ultimate sacrifice of Jesus and the gourd above his head alludes to the blood which he will shed when crucified to save mankind. Other symbols may also be seen, such as the number 6 (the six jars and six musicians) which represents the six ages of man. The hourglass on the table illustrates the passage of time.

Paolo Caliari
known as **Veronese** (1528-1588)
The Wedding Feast at Cana 1562-1563
Canvas – H 6.77 m; W 9.94 m

The Coronation of Napoléon I

Denon 8
1st floor
room 75 Daru

Go behind *The Wedding Feast at Cana.* You are now in the salon Denon, which links the rooms of the museum to the salle des Etats. In this room, art has been placed at the service of monarchy. The ceiling depicts the reigns of all those who have ruled France from Saint Louis to Napoléon I. On the right and on the left hang French paintings in large format from the nineteenth century. The rest of the collection of French paintings is on the second floor of the Sully block (see page 96). Meet on the right in the *salle Daru,* room 75.

The historic event portrayed in this painting took place on 2 December 1804 at Notre Dame Cathedral in Paris: Bonaparte, who had hitherto been First Consul, became Emperor of the French. Pope Pius VII, on the right of the painting, presides over the ceremony in which Napoléon, wreathed in laurels, crowns his wife Joséphine as Empress. There are in total more than a hundred personages present.

David took three years to complete this work. He was present at the ceremony, where he made sketches (he has pictured himself doing this in the finished painting) and carefully copied the facial expressions of the participants, in order to reproduce faithfully the reality of the occasion. Napoléon congratulated the artist and said: "This is more than a mere painting. It makes us feel as if we could enter it and walk around…". David artfully conveys the silkiness of the satin robes, the smoothness of the velvet capes edged with ermine and the sparkling shine of the diamonds. He created the perfect image of Napoleonic glory. To complete this sense of glory and encourage the belief that the Emperor's coronation was a cause for universal celebration, David also included people in his painting who were not actually at the ceremony because they disapproved of Napoléon's action.

Jacques Louis David (1748-1825)
The Coronation of Napoléon I
The 2nd of december 1804, 1806-1807
Canvas – H 6.21 m; W 9.79 m

Return to the salon
Denon, go straight
across it and enter the
Mollien room (room 77).

Théodore Géricault
(1791-1824)
The Raft of the Medusa 1819
Canvas – H 4.91 m; W 7.16 m

Denon 9
1st floor
room 77 Mollien

A group of half-naked men are huddled on a wooden raft, in the middle of a turbulent sea. A storm rages: the sky is black, the wind blows hard into the sail, and an enormous wave is about to crash on them! These are the survivors of the shipwreck of *The Medusa*, which took place in 1816 off the coast of Africa. The bodies strewn in the foreground show how many of the men died. Of the one hundred and fifty people who set out on the raft, only fifteen survived the twelve days of drifting.

The painter Géricault began work on his canvas two years after the event and chose to depict the moment when the men glimpse a ship on the horizon which might save them. They draw themselves up, full of hope, towards the figure who is waving a cloth so that the raft might be seen. But will they be found? The raft, pushed towards the left by the wind, is drifting in the opposite direction to the ship. Géricault used dark colours (black, brown, grey, dark green) to make the painting even more terrifying.

The Death of Sardanapalus

A man, lying casually on a bed, presides over a terrible scene. This huge painting recounts the suicide of a king, the cruel Sardanapalus, who according to legend lived many centuries before the birth of Christ in Nineveh, north of ancient Mesopotamia (today's Iraq). One day, his palace was besieged. Rather than surrender to the enemy, he preferred to have himself burned alive on a pyre and to order that his slaves cut the throats of all the women in his harem and those of his horses. We are shown the ruler lying on a huge bed, contemplating the massacre he has set in motion. How can he remain so calm in the face of the approaching flames (smoke is visible in the top right-hand corner)? His impassive demeanour forms a sharp contrast with the turmoil unleashed by the massacre. Around him, chaos and commotion reign. In the foreground, we can see precious objects, vases, quivers, weapons and jewels… all of which belong to Sardanapalus. This was how Western Europeans in the nineteenth century imagined the luxurious existence of a king of the East.

Delacroix hints at the massacre rather than portraying it graphically. Not a single drop of blood is visible, and yet blood dominates the painting through the abundant use of red, the colour which expresses the unleashing of the

Eugène Delacroix (1798-1863)
The Death of Sardanapalus 1827
Canvas – H 3.92 m; W 4.96 m

Denon 9
1st floor
room 77 Mollien

Go down the Mollien staircaise which is at the end of the room of the same name. You will reach the ground floor.

passions. The red in this painting streams from the top of the bed, illuminating the golden bodies of the human figures and is even reflected in the eye of the horse. We gain an impression of intense movement: the movements of the figures are in direct opposition to each other and suggest a struggle; in the bottom left-hand corner, the white horse rears up to resist the black man dragging it onto the pyre. The portrayal of the most extreme passions was a typical feature of the romantic movement.

Outside Italy, only the Louvre contains truly important works of this magnificent artist, a man of exceptional longevity who lived to the age of 89. He was at once a painter, sculptor, architect and poet, whose work during the sixteenth century actively contributed towards making the Renaissance a period of such intense creativity and artistic renewal. The two statues in the Louvre were intended for the decoration of the tomb commissioned by Pope Julius II from the most respected artist of the time. They were sculpted in an extremely simple style.

These "slaves" were given to the king of France. The one whose body is taut with effort is known as "the rebel slave", because he seems to be trying to break the chains which hold him in captivity. The other is known as "the dying slave" because he seems relaxed and ready to abandon himself to eternal sleep.

Like all Renaissance art, these works are imbued with moral significance. Do they symbolise the territories owned by the Pope? Or do they, as the artist himself claimed, represent art reduced to a state of servitude by the death of the great Pope, their protector? Or do they personify the human soul, prisoner of its passions?

Michelangelo (1475-1564)
Dying Slave
Marble – H 2.28 m

Denon 9
Ground floor
room 4

Return to the staircase and continue down to the next floor, then turn right.

Saint Marie-Madeleine

Gregor Erhart (c. 1470-1540)
Saint Marie-Madeleine,
between 1515 and 1520
Limewood – H 1.77 m; W 0.44 m

Denon 9
Entresol
room C

Retrace your steps
and turn right.

Gregor Erhart, one of the greatest sculptors of early sixteenth-century Augsburg in Germany, created a masterpiece with this work. This limewood statue represents Saint Marie-Madeleine. In the original version, placed in the choir of a church in Augsburg, she was surrounded by angels. Her bowed head, downcast eyes and distant expression convey the ecstasy of the saint transported to heaven by angels to contemplate the music of the spheres. In present times, removed from its religious context, the statue seems almost profane. The affected posture of the saint and her graceful nudity, partly concealed by voluptuous golden hair, show how the sculptor was attempting to communicate a sense of physical beauty. This was an early illustration of the spirit of the Renaissance.

Virgin and Child

Denon 9
Mezzanine
room 1,
Donatello gallery

After visiting this col-
lection, follow the
directions to the exit
in the Pyramid but
do not go down into
the main entrance
hall. Your tour conti-
nues in the Richelieu
block: cross the hall
on the mezzanine.
Take the corridor
which leads to
room 20. Turn right
and you will reach
the *cour Puget*.

Donato di Nicolo Bardi
known as **Donatello** (c. 1386-1466)
Virgin and Child
about 1440
Painted clay with gold leaf
H 1.02 m; W 0.74 m; L 0.12 m

Donatello contributed a great deal to
the development of sculpture, a new art
form which flourished during the
Italian Renaissance. Many features of
his work epitomise the rediscoveries
and creativity of the Renaissance: the
monumental size of the statuary, the
expressiveness of the faces, the sense of
perspective and the confident carving of
the bronze. The sculpture was wrought
in clay and then painted and covered
with gold leaf. The child turns from the
Virgin as though he fears she will per-
ceive the suffering he is to endure. In
terms both of its composition and the
portrayal of its subject, this work spar-
ked a complete renewal of images of the
Madonna in fifteenth century Italy.

Milo of Croton

Milo was an unbeatable wrestler from the ancient town of Croton in southern Italy. To prove his strength, he tried to break a tree in half with his bare hands, but the tree closed up again, making him its prisoner. Thus restrained, he was eaten by a wolf. In his sculpture Puget preferred to depict a lion, its enormous claws sunk into Milo's flesh. The body of the athlete is bent double in pain. All his muscles are taut, while his face is an image of suffering. The right angles between his torso and his limbs and the perpendicular diagonal lines of the sculpture accentuate its dynamic effect.

Puget was a great sculptor of the century of Louis XIV; he did not reside at Versailles, like the other artists of this period, but in Provence where he was less subject to official constraints.
Go up to the upper terrace, then go into room 28, which is slightly to the left in front of you.

The French sculpture collections provide a complete overview of French sculpture from the Middle Ages until the middle of the nineteenth century. The nucleus of the collections was formed by the works acquired during the revolutionary period. Since then they have been enriched by works from princely and other royal domains and displayed in the Tuileries gardens. To preserve some of the most prestigious works from the effects of pollution, they have been moved to the Richelieu wing.

Richelieu 3
Ground floor
cour Puget

Go up to the upper terrace, then go into room 28, which is slightly to the left in front of you.

Pierre Puget (1620-1694)
Milo of Croton
1670-83
Marble – H 2.80 m

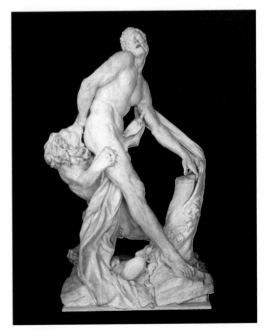

Richelieu 3
Ground floor
room 28

Jean-Antoine Houdon (1741-1828)
Louise Brongniart aged five
1777
Clay – H 0.35 m

Return to the
cour Puget.

It was Houdon's official portraits, the marble busts and statues he executed, which made him famous. Yet he also produced more personal works, in clay. Easier to work than marble and less expensive than bronze, this medium enabled him to bring individual facial expressions to life.

In this work, Louise's coiffure is coming undone, her bearing is full of life and her face has a mischievous expression. This small bust of Louise Brongniart is one example of the many portraits of children produced during this period. Houdon also sculpted busts of his wife and his daughters which can be found in the Louvre; they are perfect examples of the art of a realist sculptor working with all the freshness of youth.

Antoine-Louis Barye (1796-1875)
Lion fighting a serpent 1832-1835
Bronze – H 1.35 m; W 1.78 m

Richelieu 3
Ground floor
**cour Puget,
upper terrace**

Cross the cour
Puget, then cross
room 20 to reach the
cour Marly.

Barye, a great enthusiast of animal sculpture, took the animals in the *Jardin des Plantes* as his models. He loved cats, birds of prey and snakes, observing the cruel conflicts of nature at close quarters and making them into sculptures with all the ardour of a Romantic. Romantic artists often took human interest stories, other items of news or the natural world as the subject matter for their art. They gave priority to the free expression of feelings, often sad, savage or violent.

Barye emphasises the ferocious expression of the king of the animals. A multitude of details bear witness to the many hours he spent observing lions; the tension of the lion's muscles, the tufts of its hair, its outstretched claws pinning the serpent to the ground, all are represented as realistically as possible. This sculpture was a tribute to king Louis-Philippe, who came to power in July 1830.

Richelieu 2
Ground floor
cour Marly

From 1679 until his death in 1715, Louis XIV took great care of his residence at Marly. He had it built as a place where he could go to rest accompanied by his court favourites. When he grew tired of the lavish splendour of *le château de Versailles*, the king liked to relax in more simple surroundings. Around the house "of the sun" there were twelve small houses with magnificent gardens containing waterfalls, fountains, copses and marble statues. These houses were unfortunately destroyed at the beginning of the nineteenth century.

A team of sculptors each provided a statue, most of them inspired by ancient mythology. Some had water as their principal theme (*the Seine, the Marne, Neptune*), while some referred to Diana, the goddess of nature and hunting.

The square is overlooked by four enormous horses, each accompanied by a man. These are the famous *Horses of Marly*. The two oldest ones are *Renown* and *Mercury,* a winged horse ridden by Mercury who proclaims "whether in peace or in war, forever glory". They were sculpted by Coysevox and placed by the horses' drinking trough at Marly in 1702.

These vivid works from the end of Louis XIV's reign were all hewn from one large block of marble, a technical feat that only great sculptors could achieve. In 1719, the horses were moved to the entrance to the Tuileries gardens, by the place de la Concorde. Twenty years later, Louis XV decided to fill the empty spaces left at Marly by this move and commissioned two more statues from Guillaume 1er Coustou. During the revolutionary period, these were placed at the entrance to the Champs-Elysées, providing a counterpoint to those of Coysevox. The sculptures of Coustou show grooms taming wild horses which were meant to symbolise America and Europe. Since the time of Coysevox, the art of sculpture had greatly changed: realist works had begun to be more widely appreciated. In these sculptures we see the very real struggle between the man, his muscles taut with effort, and the bridling horse he is trying to control. To preserve them against traffic pollution, the originals of these works are now kept in the Louvre, while their original sites in Paris are taken by copies.

Antoine Coysevox (1640-1720)
Renown riding Pegasus
1699-1702
Marble – H 3.26 m

Guillaume 1ᵉʳ Coustou (1677-1746)
Horse restrained by a groom,
known as *the Horse of Marly* 1739-1745
Marble – H 3.55 m

From the upper terrace,
enter room 8 and turn right.

Richelieu 2
Ground floor
room 10

The tomb of Philippe Pot
Last quarter of the fifteenth century
Painted stone, H 1.80 m; W 2.65 m

Eight hooded figures carry on their shoulders a tombstone bearing an oustretched knight, his hands joined in prayer. This impressive funeral monument is that of seigneur de la Roche-Pot, who died in September 1493. Before becoming chamberlain in the household of king Louis XI, he was seneschal to the Duke of Burgundy, the region from which the stone for the tomb was taken.

These figures dressed in black, walking with bowed heads, their faces concealed under their hoods, are official religious mourners. Their presence recalls the great processions that used to take place at burials as the deceased were taken to their tomb. Each mourner carries a coat of arms which represents one of the eight quarters of nobility of Philippe Pot. If the mourners and their attitude of prayer suggests death and faith in God, the knight's armour and the armorial markings indicate the importance of the deceased during his life.

Diana, goddess of nature and hunting, holds her bow in her left hand; with the other she clasps a stag with impressive antlers. They are mounted on a pedestal decorated with shells and initials. This sculpture comes from the chateau of Anet, west of Paris, a sumptuous house built by the architect Philibert Delorme for Diana of Poitiers, Henri II's mistress. In one courtyard there was a huge fountain with this sculpture of Diana at the top. The sculpture was thus intended as a flattering reference to the mistress of the house. The identity of the sculptor is unknown. Many parts of the sculpture were restored or added during the nineteenth century. This kind of reclining naked figure originated in a famous artistic centre patronised by Francis I and then by his son Henri II, the chateau of Fontainebleau. As all artistic styles generally acquire names, this style was inevitably christened "Fontainebleau school". It was a refined, courtly form of art, characterised by idealised representations of the female nude.

Richelieu 2
Ground floor
room 15

Leave the French sculpture section, cross the *cour Marly* on the upper terrace and take the ministerial staircase up to first floor. At the top of the staircase, turn left.

Diana of Anet
Mid-sixteenth century
Marble – H 2.11 m

Napoléon III's apartments

In 1861, Napoléon III's apartments were used by the minister of State responsible for relations between the Government and the Assembly. They provide an exceptional illustration of the decorative arts of the Second Empire; in 1871, they were given to the Ministry of Finance, which only agreed to relinquish them in 1989. After climbing the stairs, the visitor enters a vast antechamber with walnut panelling followed by a luxurious reception room, the *Grand Salon;* its decor, which includes paintings, sculpture, rich fabrics and magnificent chandeliers, is characteristic of that period's taste for luxury, splendour and comfort. The *Grand Salon* opens into the theatre room, whose decorations have a floral and musical theme. The visitor then arrives in the small dining room which has a door through to the large dining room. This last room, hugely impressive in size, contains an imposing long dining table and a sideboard in dark wood adorned with gilded bronze.

Retrace your steps, go past the landing of the great staircase which you have just climbed, and pass through a series of rooms; to the left of a book-shop counter begin the rooms containing medieval objets d'art.

Charles the Bald's Paten is one of the masterpieces from the Cathedral of Saint-Denis. This saucer, on which the host was placed, was donated by Charles II, the Bald (king of France from 843 to 877). It is made from an ancient cup of green stone (serpentine) encrusted with golden fish. In the time of Charles the Bald the gold setting was added; into this have been placed pearls, precious stones and coloured glass, between the small ridges formed by bands of gold.

Among the most precious exhibits on show in these first four rooms of medieval objets d'art are those from the Treasury of Saint-Denis. North of Paris there is a famous cathedral, previously an abbey, which is named after the first bishop of Paris who lived in the third century. Legend has it that, beheaded at Montmartre by the Romans, Saint Denis picked up his head and carried it to the place where he wished to be buried. A church was built on this site in the fifth century. Saint Denis became protector of the kingdom and was revered by the kings of France. Their veneration expressed itself in varied ways; they might undertake reconstruction or improvement works on the cathedral, have themselves buried there, or donate magnificent gifts. These gifts became a fabulous "treasure" which people travelled from afar to admire. Unfortunately many of these objects disappeared during the Wars of Religion or during the revolutionary period (see in the same collection *The Abbey of Saint-Denis and its treasures*). (In French).

Richelieu 3
1st floor
rooms 1 à 4

Charles the Bald's Paten
1 BC or 1 AD (serpentine cup),
second half of the ninth century
(setting)
Serpentine, gold, precious stones, pearls,
coloured glass – D 0.17 m

The Sceptre of Charles V (room 4), was commissioned by Charles V for the coronation of his son Charles VI (1380-1422). The sceptre is a part of the *regalia* used during the coronation. At its tip is a small statue of Charlemagne, placed on a fleur-de-lys mounted on a circular boss which illustrates three episodes from the life of Charlemagne. Placed in the abbey of Saint-Denis, it is now on display in the Louvre with the royal spurs, the "sword of Joy" and the hand of Justice.

The Virgin with Child (room 3) was donated to Saint-Denis in 1339 by queen Jeanne of Evreux. This statuette in gold and silver stands on an intricately-worked base, decorated with fourteen enamel plaques narrating the life of Christ. The statue is carrying an iron and crystal fleur-de-lys which contains relics of the clothes, hair and milk of the Virgin.

Richelieu 3
1st floor
rooms 1 à 4

Continue on ahead
and turn right.

The Virgin of Jeanne d'Evreux
Paris, before 1339
Gilded silver, translucent enamel
on stone base – H 0.68 m

The Sceptre of Charles V
Paris, fourteenth century
Gold, pearls, precious stones
H 0.60 m

Maximilian's Hunting Scenes

This wall hanging has long been considered one of the masterpieces of sixteenth-century tapestry. It was woven in Brussels, the most important centre for the production of such art. The ensemble, a hanging, is made up of twelve sections representing episodes from hunting during various seasons of the year. It begins on the left with the month of March, considered the first month of the year at the time, which shows a panorama of the town of Brussels. In April, the episode represented is the departure for the hunt of groups of greyhounds and spaniels. May and June invite us to the preparation and the enjoyment of the hunters' meal respectively. In July the pursuit of the deer begins. August, September and October illustrate the capture of the deer, the struggle in a lake, the killing and then the giving of the quarry to the hounds. November, December and January show a hunt for wild boar, which is confronted in December by a horseman thought to resemble Maximilian I – hence the name of the hanging. In actual fact it is probably meant to be his grandson Ferdinand, brother of Charles V. February is a tribute by the huntsmen to King Modus and Queen Ratio, symbolic figures from a famous treatise on hunting written during the fourteenth century.

Richelieu 3
1st floor
room 19

After Bernard Van Orley
The month of December
(10th part of Maximilien's Hunting Scenes) Brussels, 1531-1533
Tapestry, wool and silk with threads of gold and silver – H 4.44 m; W 6.05 m

Retrace your steps, then take the escalator on your left to the second floor. Pass through the first three rooms of French paintings – you will come back to them later – and turn left. You have reached the beginning of the part of the Louvre devoted to paintings from Northern European Schools. Meet in room 4.

Van Eyck, who lived in Flanders during the 1430s, was a very famous painter in his time and was protected by Philippe le Bon, Duke of Burgundy, whose territories extended as far as Flanders (today part of Belgium). The man represented here is Nicolas Rolin, a native of Autun and an important dignitary of the court of Philippe le Bon. He gave this painting of the Virgin with Child, in which he is represented as the donor, to the collegiate church of Notre-Dame of Autun. Van Eyck was one of the very first painters to use oils in his art. With oil, the paint stands out more clearly, produces a smooth and shiny effect, and allows for greater precision in details, illustrated here by the brocade costume lined with fur, the veins in the temple of the donor, the pearls in the crown of the Virgin and the precious stones of her cloak …

The small garden is strewn with thirty different varieties of flowers, all of which are identifiable and probably carrying symbolic significance, such as the lily, symbol of the purity of the Virgin Mary. In the background we can see two lively towns linked by a bridge crossing the river; they represent the world protected by Jesus, who gives his blessing with his right hand.

Flemish, Dutch and German works made a late appearance in the royal collections. The nucleus of this collection was gathered for Louis XVI.

Richelieu 3
2nd floor
room 4

Continue on ahead. You will pass by works by Memling, Bosch and David. Meet in room 8 where German paintings of the sixteenth century are displayed.

Jan Van Eyck (d. 1441)
The Madonna of chancellor Rolin
about 1434
Wood – H 0.66 m; W 0.62 m

Self-Portrait

Albrecht Dürer (1471-1528)
Self-Portrait 1493
Parchment on canvas – H 0.57 m; W 0.45 m

Richelieu 3
2nd floor
room 8

This is one of the first works painted by Dürer, who was an important figure of the German Renaissance. He was only twenty-two years old when he painted himself holding a branch of thistle in his right hand. Some think that this is an image of marital fidelity: in this case the painting would be a present to his fiancée, whom he married in 1494. Others see religious meaning in the painting. The prickles of the thistle would thus recall those of Christ's crown of thorns. An inscription at the top of the work may be translated as follows: "The will of God shall determine my destiny".

Pieter Bruegel the Elder
(c. 1525-1569)
The Beggars 1568
Wood – H 0.19 m; W 0.22 m

Richelieu 4
2nd floor
room 10

Five men with mangled limbs seem to be going their separate ways after some kind of meeting; they are no doubt leaving to take up their begging positions in different parts of the village. This is suggested by an inscription at the top of the painting: "Cripples, may your business prosper". The work evokes the misery which may afflict man. Nevertheless, Bruegel seems to feel no pity for these unfortunates: he depicts them as grotesque creatures. This image remains a mysterious one. It could be a social allegory; the headwear of each beggar suggests that they are meant to represent a different class in society. The one wearing a cardboard crown could represent a king, the one with a paper shako a soldier, the one with the beret a bourgeois, the one with the ordinary hat a peasant and the one with the paper mitre a bishop. Nevertheless, as their bodies have all been affected by the same suffering, all are equal. Some critics have interpreted the fox tails attached to the clothes of the beggars as an emblem of support for the *parti des Gueux* (the "beggars' party"), Flemish people then engaged in a rebellion against Spanish rule.

Turn left out of room 17 and go to room 18.

The History of Marie de Médicis

Northern european schools

This is one of the most prestigious achievements in the history of painting. These works were originally displayed in the Luxembourg Palace (today occupied by the Senate), residence of Queen Marie de Médicis, wife of Henri IV, and regent of the kingdom after the assassination of the king. In this series of paintings, Marie had herself represented as a true heroine. Painted by Rubens, unaided, between 1622 and 1625, these twenty-four great canvases illustrate the principal events in the life of the queen. In order to glorify her life – without concealing the trials undergone by the queen, which reveal her courage in the face of adversity – Rubens combined real historical figures with the gods of ancient mythology: we can see an example of this in the painting portraying the moment when Henri IV receives the portrait of Marie de Médicis, whom he has never seen before. In the sky we can see Jupiter, the most powerful of all the gods, and his wife Juno, goddess of marriage. This canvas is thus attempting to suggest that the coming union between Marie and the king of France is favoured by the gods.

Pierre Paul Rubens (1577-1640)
Henri IV receiving the portrait of Marie de Médicis
Canvas – H 3.94 m; W 2.95 m

Richelieu 2
2nd floor
room 18

Return to room 17. On the left, after a door, is the Lefuel staircase, a marvel of Napoléon III style, which used to lead through to the library (destroyed by fire in 1871). Go straight ahead, go down to the landing and then up again to reach room 31.

Rembrandt, the greatest painter in the Low Countries, where he was born in 1606, was more gifted than any other in the art of conveying the nuances of human feelings and emotions. This is one of his masterpieces: he has painted an episode from the Bible. The beautiful Bethsheba was seen bathing while her husband was away by King David, who wanted to obtain her favours. He told her of his desires in a letter. The young woman is here seen holding the message, looking sad and reflective: she is already resigned to the fate that awaits her.

The painting only includes information essential to the story. Rembrandt never troubled himself with superfluous details. All our attention is drawn to Bathsheba; she stands out clearly against a shadowy background. The model, probably Rembrandt's mistress Henrickje Stoffels, has been realistically painted. The presence of the King is only suggested by the letter she is holding.

In the work of Rembrandt, as this painting illustrates so well, scenes from the Bible acquire a universal relevance; they are stories for all times, all countries, and speak to all peoples

Richelieu 3
2nd floor
room 31

Rembrandt Harmenz Van Rijn
(1606-1669)
Bathsheba bathing 1654
Canvas – H 1.42 m; W 1.42 m

The Astronomer

What is this man doing? From the instruments on his table, we can guess that he studies the stars. There is a compass, an astrolabe – used to measure the height of the stars above the horizon – and a globe representing the sky and its constellations, on which he is checking the information written in the book open on his desk.

This is indeed an astronomer at work. Vermeer lived in Delft, a small town in Holland. He liked to paint women absorbed in an activity, such as *The Lacemaker* (also in this room), bent over her work. His fine understanding of the effects of light enabled him to make simple scenes into something much more than the banal representation of daily life.

A quiet atmosphere pervades this painting. The world of Vermeer is that of silence and internal life. Through the window on the left there filters a gentle, golden light which illuminates the globe, caresses the astronomer's face and melts into the soft Eastern carpet. When we approach the painting, we can see how the artist has used small juxtaposed dots of paint to create the impression of light shining on the globe and on the carpet.

Richelieu 3
2nd floor
room 38

Continue on ahead, past the escalator. Again you reach the beginning of the collection of French paintings.

Johannes Vermeer (1632-1675)
The Astronomer 1668
Canvas – H 0.50 m; W 0.45 m

The Louvre's collection of French paintings is exceptional in its quality and comprehensiveness. The royal collections begun by Louis XIV form its core; these were then complemented by works seized during the revolutionary period, and later acquisitions, bequests and donations.

Richelieu 3
2nd floor
room 1

This portrait, painted on a panel of oak, is extremely famous: it is one of the oldest French paintings to have survived to the present day; it is also the earliest example in Europe of a portrait of a single individual. It is undoubtedly a portrait of Jean le Bon, King of France between 1350 and 1364 and father of Charles V. The ruler is pictured without his crown, maybe because he was not yet king at the time the portrait was executed, but still the Duke of Normandy. The inscription "Jehan roy de France" ("Jean King of France") was probably added later. The artist who painted this portrait, whose name is unknown, attempted to make it resemble its subject, without embellishing the monarch's features.

Anonymous
Portrait of Jean le Bon
about 1350
Wood – H 0.60 m; W 0.45 m

Portrait of Charles VII

French paintings

Jean Fouquet (c. 1420 - c. 1478/1481)
Portrait of Charles VII
about 1445-1450
Wood – H 0.86 m; W 0.71 m

Richelieu 3
2ⁿᵈ floor
room 6

Jean (c. 1485-1541)
and François (1505/1510-1572) **Clouet**
Portrait of Francis I about 1530
Wood – H 0.96 m; W 0.74 m
room 7

Jean Fouquet, the greatest French painter of the fifteenth century, painted this portrait of Charles VII, "the most victorious King of France". He reigned from 1422 to 1461, and with the help of Joan of Arc, liberated France from English occupation. In this work Fouquet invented a new image of royalty. The evolution in the art of the portrait since that of Jean le Bon is evident. In this work, we can see the king's entire upper body, which is almost facing the onlooker. The image is imposing: the king's face stands out clearly between the triangles formed by the drapes and the clothes on his body.

The painter probably acquired his interest in geometric forms from Italian Renaissance painters, whose work he studied during a visit to Italy. On the other hand, the king's face is not at all stylised; it is realistically portrayed, as it would be by the painters of the Flemish school. This work was extremely influential on future royal portraits. This can be seen in the next room in the portrait of Francis I painted by Jean and François Clouet: the king's outfit is more luxurious, but it is clear that they used Fouquet's work during the previous century as a model.

97

Gabrielle d'Estrées and one of her sisters

French paintings

Anonymous
*Gabrielle d'Estrées
and one of her sisters* about 1594
Wood – H 0.96 m; W 1.25 m

Richelieu 3
2nd floor
room 10

Two women in a bath, one of whom pinches the nipple of the other – quite an amazing double portrait. On the right is Gabrielle d'Estrées, mistress of Henri IV; we can deduce from the title of the painting that the woman on the left is her sister, the Duchess of Villars. A servant stands in the background. The action of the Duchess of Villars is an allusion to the fact that Gabrielle had recently given birth to a child.

In 1594 she gave birth to César de Vendôme, the illegitimate son of Henri IV. The ring which she holds between two fingers alludes to her relationship with the king.

This kind of subject, the upper body of a naked woman in her bath, was perfected by François Clouet. The nudity, the elegance of the human figures and their delicate gestures make this work part of the Fontainebleau school.

A Concert

Valentin de Boulogne
known as **le Valentin** (1591-1632)
A Concert about 1628-30
Canvas – H 1.75 m; W 2.16 m

Richelieu 3
2nd floor
room 11

Some French artists who visited Rome at the beginning of the seventeenth century found the city a new source of inspiration. Rome was an active artistic centre where Caravaggio (1571-1610) exerted considerable influence on these young French painters. He painted realistic scenes (see page 66) and used the effects of light in contrast with dark shadows – chiaroscuro – to make his painting more striking.

Valentin de Boulogne, like other French artists, was struck by the power of the art of the Roman master. Like Caravaggio, he painted genre scenes and episodes from the Bible; the human figures in his paintings emerge from the shadows in a highly dramatic manner, while their thoughtful, worried faces suggest the painter was of a passionate temperament and had an anguished view of humanity.

The Judgement of Solomon

Nicolas Poussin (1594-1665)
The Judgement of Solomon 1649
Canvas – H 1.01 m; W 1.50 m

Richelieu 3
2nd floor
room 14

Two women are engaged in a violent struggle. They have been living in the same house; each of them had a baby, but one of the babies died. Brought before Solomon, the wise king of the Bible, both claim to be the mother of the surviving child. The king orders the baby to be cut in half, so that each woman might have half. A soldier prepares to kill it. The woman on the left, terrified, screams that she will abandon her claim to the child if the king allows it to live. The other woman, her face twisted with hate, prefers the child to be cut in two. The real mother must be the one who has given up her right to the baby so that it might be spared.

Solomon thus decides to return the child to her, alive.

Poussin successfully expresses the drama of the story through the posture of the characters, the expressions on their faces, and by his use of colour. The king is clothed in red and white, colours that symbolise power and justice. To paint the bad mother, Poussin uses muted colours: her green complexion underlines her cruelty. By contrast, the good mother is wearing luminous clothes of yellow with touches of blue and orange, colours which represent intelligence and wisdom.

The Four Seasons

French paintings

Nicolas Poussin (1594-1665)
Spring 1660-4
Canvas – H 1.18 m; W 1.60 m

Richelieu 3
2nd floor
room 16

Turn left towards
French paintings
of the seventeenth
to the nineteenth
century

Each of these four paintings represents a particular season and a particular time of day. Each one also recounts a story from the Bible. In the first painting, a beautiful spring morning takes us to paradise on earth. Adam and Eve, the first humans created by God, live alone in green countryside.

Then comes summer and the hottest part of the day. We are taken to a large corn field where peasants are busying themselves with their crops. Booz, the owner of the estate, allows a poor woman, Ruth, to keep some of her corn for herself.

The third painting evokes the end of an autumn afternoon. It is the time of harvest. One bunch of grapes is so heavy it takes two men to carry it. It is the fruit of a unique place – the promised land.

Finally comes winter, a bleak landscape on a tragic night. God has decided that mankind must be punished and decides to eliminate it from the Earth by unleashing forty days of rain. This was the time of the Flood. Only Noah and his family were spared from death by drowning.

The Sermon of Saint Paul

During the seventeenth century, painters received many commissions for paintings to decorate churches and monasteries. One of the most important commissions was that of the "May paintings"; every year from 1630 to 1707, artisans would donate a huge painting to Notre-Dame Cathedral in Paris. These works were shown to the public from 1 May onwards. For painters, an order for a May painting was a chance for them to have their talent recognised by all. These paintings were taken down and dispersed during the revolutionary period.

The *Sermon of St. Paul at Ephesea,* painted by Eustache Le Sueur, is one such painting. In the centre, the apostle Paul is preaching in the Greek town of Ephesea. The strength of his belief will ensure that its inhabitants convert to the Christian religion.
They are gathering around him in order to burn the books of the old religion. Le Sueur puts great emphasis on the figure of the apostle: dressed in red and placed in the centre of the painting, he dominates the entire scene.

Sully 4
2nd floor
room 19

Eustache Le Sueur (1616-1655)
The Sermon of St. Paul at Ephesea
1649
Canvas – H 3.94 m; W 3.28 m

Sully 4
2nd floor
room 27

Lubin Baugin
(c. 1612-1663)
Still Life with Chessboard
Wood – H 0.55 m; W 0.73 m

A still life painting contains objects such as flowers, fruit, vegetables, game or fish. The way in which these objects are represented can conceal a hidden meaning: this is the case in this work, which alludes to the five senses: sight (the mirror), hearing (the musical instrument), smell (the carnations), touch (the money contained in the purse, the chessboard and the card game) and taste (the bread and the glass of wine). Strangely, the mirror is black and reflects nothing; it is there to remind us that all the objects in the painting, which evoke life and its pleasures, may one day disappear – the day we die. This kind of work was often known as a vanitas. At a time when religious feeling was extremely powerful, such paintings encouraged the onlooker to abandon the vanity of worldly goods and move closer to God, the only guarantee of eternal life.

Georges de La Tour (1593-1652)
The Cheat with the ace of diamonds
about 1630
Canvas – H 1.06 m; W 1.46 m

This naïve-looking young man, on the right, runs the risk of having the gold pieces in front of him stolen. The character on the left is preparing to cheat, by using an ace of diamonds he has hidden in his belt. The woman sitting in the middle, probably a courtesan, is his accomplice – we can tell from her side glance and from her hand oustretched to receive the ace – as is the servant, who is carrying a glass of wine intended to dull the awareness of their victim. This painting is more than an amusing anecdote; it warns the young of the dangers of wine, women and gambling.

During the first half of the seventeenth century, the theme of card-players was extremely fashionable among painters who, throughout Europe, had been influenced by the Italian Caravaggio (1571-1610). This innovative artist liked to paint scenes from ordinary life, even in his religious paintings (see page 66).

The brightness of the colours and the pale complexions of the faces are reinforced by the dark background and by the daylight shining through from the left. There is a huge contrast in the other canvasses of Georges de La Tour between daylight scenes and those which are illuminated by candlelight.

Louis Le Nain
(c. 1600/1610-1648)
Peasant Family 1642
Canvas – H 1.13 m; W 1.59 m

The Le Nain brothers, Antoine, Louis and Mathieu, were all painters. They all signed their work with their surname only, thus making it difficult to attribute their paintings to any one of them in particular.

In this famous *Peasant Family,* the artist barely includes the house where the scene takes place at all; he prefers to concentrate on the human figures, who are immobile and thoughtful. The range of colours used is extremely limited: the shades of brown and grey accurately reflect the austerity of life in the countryside. They convey an impression of calm. The Le Nain brothers deliberately used earthen colours to express the humble character of this family.

These peasants are not rich, their house is a simple one, their children have no shoes. But all this does not mean that they live in misery. They are decently clothed and do not appear to be hungry. The peasant woman on the left is even holding a very elegant stemmed glass. The dignified and serious nature of the scene is slightly attenuated by the amusing detail of the cat hiding behind a pot.

The Battles of Alexander

Charles Le Brun (1619-1690)
The Battle of Arbelles 1669
Canvas – H 4.70 m; W 12.64 m

Sully 5
2nd floor
room 32

The four immense canvasses which Le Brun painted between 1665 and 1673 depict four episodes from the the *History of Alexander,* the famous conqueror of Ancient Greece, to whom Louis XIV liked to be compared. Appointed first painter to the King in 1664, and an active member of the powerful Royal Academy of Painting and Sculpture founded in 1648, Charles Le Brun was given responsibility by the minister Colbert for the decoration of the royal chateaux, most notably that of Versailles. It was his task to direct all the artists involved in the decoration and to co-ordinate all their work into a lavish yet dignified style, now known as *style Louis XIV*. This series of works was of considerable importance in the definition of the academic style taught by Le Brun. *The Battle of Arbelles,* a canvas full of action and drama, shows Alexander, his sword raised, trying to catch Darius, his Persian enemy, who is seated in his chariot; the terrified Darius prepares to leave his throne to mount the horse offered to him by a soldier. Behind Alexander, the dervish Aristendes points out the eagle flying above the prince as a sign of victory. In the distance, Alexander's camp is being attacked by Persians.

Portrait of Louis XIV

French paintings

Hyacinthe Rigaud (1659-1743)
Portrait of Louis XIV 1701
Canvas – H 2.77 m; W 1.94 m

Sully 5
2nd floor
room 34

This canvas was originally painted for King Philip V of Spain, Louis XIV's grandson, but it became so widely admired that it was retained in France. With this portrait, in which the pomp and majesty of the Sun-King are on full display, Rigaud created the perfect image of the absolute monarch. Louis XIV, aged sixty-three at the time, is represented against a background of solemn wall-hangings. Dressed in full ceremonial costume, he is pictured with all the emblems of royalty: a fleur-de-lys cloak with ermine borders, the "Sword of Joy", the sceptre and the hand of Justice. Only the head was painted in the actual presence of the king; the rest of the picture was painted in the studio of the artist, who then painted the face of Louis XIV onto the canvas.

Sully 5
2nd floor
room 36

Jean-Antoine Watteau
(1684-1721)
Pierrot about 1718-1719
Canvas – H 1.84 m; W 1.49 m

When Louis XIV died, his great-grandson, the future Louis XV, was only five years old. Until he came of age in 1723, Philippe d'Orléans, Louis XIV's nephew, ruled over the kingdom: this was the period of the Regency during which people were ready for more imagination and flights of fancy: social norms became more relaxed. In painting, less serious subject matter began to be appreciated. This was the beginning of the rococo era.

Pierrot is a character from the Comédie-Italienne. 1718, the year Watteau painted his picture, was a year when Pierrot and his companions such as Harlequin would regularly entertain Parisians with their music, mime, dance and song. The world of the theatre often inspired Watteau, notably famous for his "fêtes galantes", paintings depicting meetings of lovers in idyllic verdant settings. This portrayal of Pierrot is a touching one. Standing rigidly upright, with his arms dangling, he seems intimidated. His role in the drama was often one of an innocent and dreamer who simply enjoyed playing the guitar. Behind him we can see his companions, the Doctor on his donkey, Leander, Isabelle and the Captain. It is generally thought that this work was painted for the actor Belloni, who, after gaining fame in the *commedia dell'arte,* bought a café which could have had this painting as its sign.

The Skate

Jean Siméon Chardin
(1699-1779)
The Skate about 1725-6
Canvas – H 1.14 m; W 1.46 m

Sully 5
2nd floor
room 38

When Chardin's painting was first put on public display, the realism of the scene greatly shocked his contemporaries. We are faced by an enormous skate, red with blood, hanging from a hook. In front of it, on the wooden table, Chardin has painted various household tools side by side, such as a jug, a knife, a skimmer, a saucepan and a copper cauldron; on the left, he has painted dead fish, oysters and leeks. The cat is the only living thing present, prowling among the oysters. The skate seems to be looking out of the picture, but in fact its ears and not its eyes are facing the onlooker.

When we approach the painting, we notice from close up that the stomach of the skate is painted with small brushstrokes of white paint; if we observe it from afar, it seems shiny and silver, as if it had only just been caught. Again, close to the picture we can see that the insides of the oysters are made up of large brushstrokes of white paint; from a distance we can see the mother of pearl through the transparent fresh water. By looking at each part of the painting in this way, we can see that none of its component elements is inert, everything in it is alive and moving.

The Dejeuner

The Dejeuner and Grace depict particular moments of daily life; they are genre scenes. Boucher's canvas shows a family about to have coffee. In Chardin's painting, a young girl says her prayers (*Le Bénédicité*, the painting's French title, refers to the word *benedicite*, the first Latin word of the prayer said before a meal). These works are valuable documents for understanding what life was like in the eighteenth century. Through them we can discover the furnishings and fashions of the time. In *The Dejeuner*, on the left of the picture, a porcelain figure – a Chinese magot – illustrates the enthusiasm at the time for objects from the East; we can also see a clock and a lamp with complicated designs, items which were fashionable in the first half of the eighteenth century.

These paintings are more than historical documents; they also reflect the individual style and vision of each artist. According to our tastes, we might prefer either the delicate and peaceful scene evoked by Chardin, or the comfortable intimacy of the Parisian family painted by Boucher, which may be his own family.

François Boucher (1703-1770)
The Dejeuner 1739
Canvas – H 0.82; W 0.67 m

Sully 5
2nd floor
room 40

Before continuing on to room 48, turn left into room 42, the curiously named "chicken corridor", where there are works in pastel and delightful miniatures on display. This corridor provides a magnificent view over the Seine and in the distance, the Panthéon can be seen. We are now behind the Perrault colonnade, the eastern façade of the Louvre, built under Louis XIV, which faces the church of St. Germain-l'Auxerrois.

Jean-Baptiste Siméon Chardin
(1699-1779)
Grace 1740
Canvas – H 0.50 m; W 0.39 m

Jean Honoré Fragonard (1732-1806)
Fancy face 1769
Canvas – H 0.80 m; W 0.65 m

Sully 6
2nd floor
room 48

The "Fancy faces" are a series of paintings depicting characters dressed in Spanish costumes. The Louvre has eight such paintings in its possession. They are portraits of clients or of friends which may have been brought together by Fragonard in the lodgings he possessed at the Louvre. In this painting we are in the presence of the abbé de Saint-Non, one of Fragonard's main patrons. On the back of the picture, an old label tells us that the work was completed "in one hour".

When we move closer to the canvas, we can see (especially in the clothes and hands of the abbé) the traces of long brushstrokes.

This shows the speed with which they were applied to the canvas. This kind of portrait was quite new: contrary to the traditions of portraiture, Fragonard did not try to reproduce faithfully the features of his model. His main concern was to try and capture the fleeting expression of the character at a specific moment.

Hubert Robert (1733-1808)
The Pont du Gard 1786
Canvas – H 2.42 m; W 2.42 m

Sully 6
2nd floor
room 48

During his youth, Hubert Robert spent ten years in Rome, where he was greatly moved by the remains of buildings from Ancient times. He made his name through innumerable drawings and paintings of buildings and ruined monuments, both real ones and imaginary ones. He returned to France in 1765 and until the end of his life he continued to paint Italian landscapes and buildings, working from memory. The artist was commissioned by Louis XVI to paint four paintings on the theme of famous ancient monuments for a room in the royal chateau at Fontainebleau. He chose to paint the Gallo-Roman remains of the south of France: the monuments at Nîmes, Orange, Saint-Rémy and the pont du Gard, the famous aqueduct built in 19 B.C. to provide Nîmes with drinking water. Notice how Robert uses the effects of light and shade on stone to bring these imposing arches to life.

Sully 7
2nd floor
room 60

Jean-Auguste-Dominique Ingres
(1780-1867)
Turkish bath 1862
Canvas on wood – H 1.10 m; W 1.10 m

These bathers, each a marvellous study of the female body within the lascivious atmosphere of a harem, were painted by Ingres when he was eighty-two years old. The sensuality emanating from this languid assembly of bodies constitutes the fulfilment of life-long attempts by the artist, begun fifty years earlier, to combine the female nude with the exotic atmosphere of the East. These women are the purest example of the nineteenth century Western mind's fantasies of an erotic and perfumed Eastern world.

Ingres's style was characterised by accurate observation of his models, a taste for precise detail and, at the same time, a desire to go beyond mere "realism" to achieve harmony of form. This led him to stylise much of his work and is the reason why in this picture he gave a smooth and uniform look to the women, distorting their true appearance.

Souvenir of Mortefontaine

Jean-Baptiste-Camille Corot
(1796-1875)
Souvenir of Mortefontaine,
Salon of 1864
Canvas – H 0.65 m; W 0.89 m

Corot, one of the first painters to paint directly from nature, also used to compose landscapes in his studio from studies he had made in the open air. This landscape, painted around 1864, was produced using such a technique. In it he depicts people picking fruit on the banks of the lakes of Mortefontaine, near Senlis, in an unreal and poetic atmosphere of luminous mist. The work achieves a perfect visual balance as a result of the diagonal lines of the dark tree branches which counterpoint the bushy mass of silver leaves and provide a contrast to the reflection of the cloudy sky in the water. The sense of peace emanating from this painting is due to the intelligent use of the colours green, grey-blue and white, which together create an atmosphere of tranquillity.

Sully 7
Entresol

Take the lift down from room B, or take the Henri II staircase, to the entresol, on the same level as the exit, to finish this tour with a visit to the remains of the Medieval Louvre.

The moats, with the Taillerie tower in the foreground

The construction of the Louvre began eight hundred years ago. Before becoming one of the greatest museums in the world, the Louvre was a fortress, and then the palace of the kings of France. A relief map of the Louvre in the fourteenth century (during the reign of Charles V, king of France from 1364 to 1380) shows its condition more than one hundred and fifty years after its construction was begun by king Philippe Auguste who reigned from 1180 to 1223. The Louvre was a fortress with a tower in each corner and two gates, one facing east towards Paris, one facing south towards the Seine.

Philippe Auguste had the Louvre built to defend the western approach to Paris and so placed it at the town's furthest western edge, outside the rampart which he built at the same time. Charles V enlarged Paris and had another rampart built; its moat can be seen towards the Louvre shopping centre. The king never lived in this fortress, preferring his palace which used to be on the Ile de la Cité, on the site occupied today by the Palais de Justice. This castle and its rampart have been demolished, but the foundations discovered in 1985 can be seen.

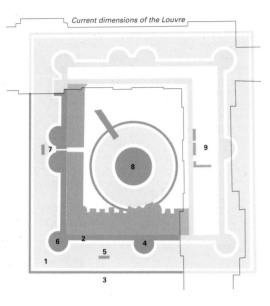

Current dimensions of the Louvre

Continue ahead
to view the founda-
tions.

*Model of the Louvre
in the time of Philippe Auguste*
Can be seen in the rooms dedicated
to the history of the Louvre
(see p. 119)

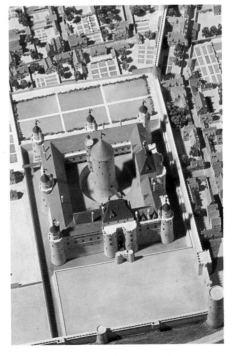

**Section of the archeological
crypt of the Cour Carrée
of the Louvre**

1 **Ditches**
   Visitors may now walk here;
   they used to be full of water
   and known as moats.

2 **Northern outer wall
   of the chateau
   of Philippe Auguste**
   Only remains survive.

3 **Counterscarp wall**
   This was next to the ditch on
   the side of the Paris city walls.

4 **Central Tower**
   This owes its name to
   its position in the centre
   of the northern wall.

5 **Support pillar
   of the drawbridge built
   under Charles V**

6 **La Taillerie Tower**
   Many of the huge bricks in this
   tower are engraved with hearts:
   these are the marks left by the
   stonecutters who were paid
   according to the number of
   bricks they had cut.

7 **Support pillar of the main
   east-facing drawbridge**
   This entrance allowed access to
   the town from the chateau.

8 **Philippe-Auguste's dungeon**

9 **Saint-Louis room**

Before even becoming king around 1362, the future Charles V began transforming the Louvre into a luxurious palace; high turrets, ornate chimneys, beautiful windows and terraces were added to make the old fortress a little more elegant. In the tower of Books, the king installed his personal library, which contained more than nine hundred manuscripts. This precious collection was stolen during the Hundred Years War. At the foot of the chateau there were gardens, a vegetable garden, a farmyard and even a menagerie with lions. Charles V had a new rampart built: this time, the Louvre was on the inside. Enlarged and improved, the chateau thus became a palace suitable for the kings of France. A huge covered tower in the shape of a cone, the tomb of Philippe-Auguste, rises up from the middle of the central courtyard (it is visible on the illumination opposite). To view the tower, take a narrow passage on the right at the end of the moat.

The Great Tower used to be thirty one metres high but now measures only seven. As it was the most secure part of the fortress, it was used to store food supplies and weapons. It was the symbol of the State until Francis I ordered its demolition in 1528.

Beyond the dungeon, we reach another room, the Saint-Louis room, on the left, where objects discovered during the excavations of 1984-5 are on display

Charles V (1364-1380)
Stone – H 1.95 m
Louvre Museum,
Department of sculpture.

The Limbourg brothers
The duc de Berry at leisure
Between 1413 and 1416.
Detail of a section of tapestry representing the month of October showing an idealised vision of the Louvre of Charles V. Chantilly, Condé Museum.

The Saint-Louis room is in all probability a room from the apartments of Philippe-Auguste which was used by the guards. In a display cabinet there are fragments of the parade helmet, or "golden hat" of king Charles VI; these were found at the bottom of a well where they had been abandoned by burglars.

Workshop of Jean Goujon
The Priest
about 1560-1564

Saint-Louis room

Exit
We leave the Louvre through a passageway that runs between the display cabinets, then down the staircase to the Pyramid. As we leave we cross a thick wall which was the base for the bridge built in the seventeenth century, during the reign of Louis XIV, by the architect Le Vau. This bridge crossed the moat of the Louvre. You will pass six large low reliefs which originally decorated the last floor of one of the facades of the Cour carrée. They were built by the great Renaissance sculptor Jean Goujon and his team of helpers, commissioned to do the work by Charles IX. On either side of a rotunda there are two exhibition rooms recounting the history of the Louvre.

LOUVRE

Réunion
des Musées
Nationaux

Musée du Louvre, Paris, 1998
Collection Chercheurs d'art

**Conceived, co-ordinated
and created by:**
Violaine Bouvet-Lanselle,
department of culture

Graphics conceived by:
Agathe Hondré,
Louvre Museum
Supervision, Philippe Apeloig

Edition secretary:
Cécile Dufêtre,
Louvre Museum

Acknowledgements to the
curators of the
Louvre museum

Illustrations:
Isabelle Gaëtan,
department of culture

**Louvre graphics workshop
co-ordinator:**
Anne-Louise Cavillon,
Louvre Museum

**Supervisor of manufactu-
ring at the RMN:**
Jacques Venelli

Translated by:
Jonathan Watson
and Mary Windsor

**Photographic
acknowledgements:**
M. Chassat / musée du Louvre,
couverture, p. 4, 5; DR, p. 117;
Giraudon, p. 118; C. Larrieu /
musée du Louvre, p. 49;
E. Revault / musée du Louvre,
p. 20, 40, 116, 119; RMN: p. 6,
8, 12, 15, 16, 34, 37, 40, 41, 48,
51, 56, 60, 61, 64, 66, 67, 69, 71,
73, 75, 77, 79, 86-91, 96, 97, 100,
101, 104, 106, 107, 109, 111,
112, 116, 118, 119; RMN /
J. Arnaudet: p. 14, 55, 57, 74,
88, 110; RMN / J.G. Berizzi:
p. 62; RMN / G. Blot: p. 10, 18,
58, 59, 65, 84, 102, 103, 113;
RMN / G. Blot / P. Jean: p. 80, 85,
114; RMN / G. Blot /
J. Schormans: p. 99; RMN /
Chuzeville: p. 21, 25, 27, 28, 31,
35, 36, 38, 39; RMN / P. Jean:
p. 92, 98, 105; RMN / C. Larrieu:
p. 30; RMN / H. Lewandowski:
p. 7, 9, 11, 13, 17, 19, 22, 23, 24,
26, 29, 33, 43-47, 50, 53, 54, 63,
97; RMN / H. Lewandowski /
P. Jean: p. 93; RMN / R.G. Ojeda:
p. 76, 78, 83, 95, 115; RMN /
R.G. Ojeda / P. Néri: p. 81;
RMN / C. Rose: 52; RMN /
J. Schormans: p. 94, 108.

Photoengraving:
I.G.S. – CP Angoulême

© Éditions de la Réunion
des musées nationaux,
Paris 1998
49 rue Étienne Marcel
75001 Paris

Printed in March 2000
by Aubin printing services Ltd

Registration of copyright:
February 1998, March 2000
ISSN 1142-334 X
ISBN 2-7118-3654-1
JC 20 3654